A FRESHMAN SURVIVAL GUIDE FOR COLLEGE STUDENTS WITH AUTISM SPECTRUM DISORDERS

A FRESHMAN SURVIVAL GUIDE FOR COLLEGE STUDENTS WITH AUTISM SPECTRUM DISORDERS

The Stuff Nobody Tells You About!

HALEY MOSS

FOREWORD BY SUSAN J. MORENO

Jessica Kingsley *Publishers*
London and Philadelphia

First published in 2014
by Jessica Kingsley Publishers
73 Collier Street
London N1 9BE, UK
and
400 Market Street, Suite 400
Philadelphia, PA 19106, USA

www.jkp.com

Library of Congress Cataloging in Publication Data
Moss, Haley.
 A freshman survival guide for college students with autism spectrum disorders : the
stuff nobody tells
you about / Haley Moss ; foreword by Susan J. Moreno.
    pages cm
 Includes index.
 ISBN 978-1-84905-984-8 (alk. paper)
1. College students with disabilities. 2. Autism spectrum disorders. 3. College
student orientation I.
Title.
 LC4818.38.M67 2014
 371.9'0474--dc23
                            2013048201

British Library Cataloguing in Publication Data
A CIP catalogue record for this book is available from the British Library

ISBN 978 1 84905 984 8
eISBN 978 0 85700 922 7

Printed and bound in the United States

To my parents, Rick and Sherry Moss.

Without everything you do, this book would never be possible, so it is only natural to have this book in your honor!

I love you both to Pluto and back, and then some.

CONTENTS

FOREWORD

Few experiences in life are more stressful, hopeful, exiting and terrifying than the contemplation of seeking higher education. This is even more intense when an autism spectrum challenge is thrown into the mix. As students on the autism spectrum and their families examine the possibility of college study and begin the selection, application and preparation for a college experience, they need all the help and advice they can get. *A Freshman Survival Guide for College Students with Autism Spectrum Disorders* is a gem of help and hope in that process. Individuals on the spectrum, their families and their advisors will all benefit from Haley's thoughts and experiences. Perhaps the most valuable aspect of this book is that Haley is living this experience as she writes about it. She admits that there are aspects in which she turns to others for advice, such as financial plans. Therefore, she avoids a trend I've seen in way too many non-spectrum (NS) experts' books in which they claim to know all aspects of their subject equally well.

Since the day I first heard Haley Moss speak publicly (which was the first time I ever met or knew of her), I have referred to Haley Moss as "our little comet"—an obvious reference to Halley's Comet, which is almost as rare a phenomenon as Haley Moss herself.

Haley is warm, friendly, smart, beautiful, and extremely talented. She is already known for her artwork. Using anime art style, Haley has produced a large number of artworks that are in high demand. She has become the spokesperson for several corporations and organizations. In addition, her first book on middle school was a huge hit. If you've never heard Haley speak in public, try to find an opportunity to do so. She is a lovely presenter.

Once again, Haley has let us into her world, her experiences and her efforts to cope with the challenges of the current phase of her life: college. Her style of writing feels like Haley is talking directly to the reader. She shares both victories and stumbles—joys and challenges—in this work.

Just reading the chapter headings will indicate to all that this is a thorough look at the subject of attending college. From deciding to try, to selecting where to apply, to applications and essays, to financial considerations, general preparations, and actually beginning the process, Haley shares her experiences and concerns.

College can be a wonderful experience for learning and social growth. Haley is doing all she can to get the maximum benefit in both areas. My own daughter who has autism was able to complete both a Bachelor's and Master's degree within the "regular" college system. When she emerged, she had grown not only in knowledge and social skills, but she had made leaps and bounds in maturity and self-help skills. I can see that Haley is well on her way to doing the same.

Since Haley has both high intelligence and a great work ethic, she is scheduled to graduate early from the University of Florida. I'm sure that graduate school education is already on her radar. Sit back and enjoy this wonderful reading experience. After all, how often do you get to follow the trail of a comet!

Susan J. Moreno
CEO and Founder, OASIS@MAAP, MAAP Services
for Autism and Asperger Syndrome

ACKNOWLEDGMENTS

I would first like to thank my parents, Sherry and Rick Moss, for all of their love, support, guidance, and so many countless other things that they have done for me throughout my life each and every day. I know that I cannot thank you enough for all of the things you have done for the past 19 years with me. Without my parents and their undying hope, determination, and encouragement, I would not be where I am today. My parents are the best people out there. Thank you for always believing in me even when I begin not to believe in myself. Because of you I never gave up no matter how big my doubts could be. You empower me every day and are nothing short of amazing. I love you to Pluto and back, and I always will.

I also want to say thank you to the rest of my family for all of their support: grandparents, uncles, aunts, cousins, and everyone else in between. I love each and every one of you, and thank you for staying by my side through thick and thin. No matter what, we are family and we are in this together.

Thank you to the wonderful team at Jessica Kingsley Publishers for allowing this book to happen. Without them, you, the reader, would not get to be reading this! I would like to specifically thank Emily McClave for believing in my vision for this book right from the start and allowing it to come to the place it is today. Thank you to the entire JKP family for all of the time and effort you put into this book and for making my dream a reality. It has been a pleasure working with everyone at

JKP, and I couldn't be more thankful to have worked with you on this book.

I would like to thank all the wonderful people and organizations I have had the chance to work with over the years to help raise autism awareness, fundraise for, write and create for, and form friendships with. Thank you to my families at Unicorn Children's Foundation, Dan Marino Foundation, Project Lifesaver International, University of Miami Center for Autism and Related Disabilities (CARD), Special-Ism, MAAP Services, and Asperkids for all you do to help our community across the world, and thank you for allowing me to join forces with you. Special thanks to Susan J. Moreno at MAAP for agreeing to write the forward for this book, and for being a fabulous mentor and friend for the last five years!

Thank you to the many Gators I have met at the University of Florida over the past two years for helping with my transition to college, being supportive of me, and just being a part of something bigger here in the Gator nation together. Thank you to Alex Nelson, who has been my best friend since we first met in the dorms right away during freshman year. You always have my back, no matter what, and have always been there for me. I know without you I would not have made it through a lot of difficult moments, and you have been nothing but amazing in being a supportive friend. A big thank you to Carolynn Komanski, who made sure my transition was friendly, and who went way above and beyond to make sure I was happy and helped me with all of my housing stuff. Go Gators!

I would like to thank you and all of the awesome people I have met over the years through the publication of my first book, my artwork, and through my philanthropy with HaleyMossART. Thank you to each and every one of you who has sent me a personal message and reached out to me. It continually excites me knowing that I have made a difference for you. Your words inspire me to keep doing what I am doing and make my days on a regular basis. Thank you to my Facebook fans for following my journey throughout the past couple of years. Thank you to anyone who ever met me at a charity event, a book signing, or an autism event for taking the time to speak with me. You are all special people to me and have a place in my heart.

And finally—thank you, the reader, for choosing to read my book and taking the time to listen to what I have to say. I might not know you or your situation, but thank you for making the effort and taking the time to read this book. Your support means the world to me, and I am forever grateful that you are interested in what I have to say. We are all in this journey of colleges, universities, and life beyond that together, and I am happy to be your companion this time.

Love always,
Haley

INTRODUCTION

Dear Reader,

First off, thank you so much for picking up this book! It is very nice to meet you. I'm not sure if you're in high school, in college, or a parent of a high school or college student, but I have a feeling that during this journey we will eventually become friends, as I share with you some experiences and advice for college! I'll try my best to be a good friend to you by giving you honest advice, listening, and not judging you during this difficult time of life: the way end of high school, right before college, and time in college.

College is supposed to be a time filled with discovery, education, friendship, independence, and so many other elements that it could easily be overwhelming or confusing to a person with an Autism Spectrum Disorder (ASD), or anyone for that matter. It sure was for me! Someone told me college is supposed to be the "best four years of your life," and you might feel like you have the obligation and expectation to feel that way, too. However, if you don't, I would like to tell you that it is completely okay not to feel like college is your prime.

"Why is she writing about college?" you may ask, and, "Who exactly are you, Haley?" I am a 19-year-old rising sophomore (or by the time you get to read this, a rising junior) with High-Functioning Autism (HFA) at the University of Florida. I just finished my freshman year of college after a lot of hard work, stress, anxiety, and some fun and excitement too, and I thought it would be a good time to get you prepared for college. In order to give you some insight into my thought process, I think I should share some background story with you.

Before I went off to college for my freshman year, I read a ton of literature about going to college: I read articles online, other books, and would ask older students I knew who were also on the autism spectrum for some of their experiences. Even with all of that research, I did not feel as if I was adequately informed about what was to lie ahead for me. No one really tells you the good, the bad, and the ugly. The most popular things that the media and others have shared are all the great things (hence why I felt obligated to have the "best four years of my life"), or the scary horror stories of drunken, nightmare roommates and stolen goods. After having too much outside, irrelevant information to interpret, and still having a feeling of unpreparedness, I thought I would take it upon myself to try my best to relay everything, no matter if it was good, bad, or ugly, to you.

I hope that, with this book, you are able to get a clear idea of what goes on at colleges and universities today. Parents, the college experience you had isn't the same as your child might have: your child has to deal with Facebook, people who aren't interacting face-to-face as much, and the new direction of education and society. It isn't easy being a college student today. As a current student, I'm able to tell you what's really happening. I feel like I go through school as a secret agent and am reporting back to you on what you should know so you have a smooth transition from high school to college, and are prepared for anything that comes your way!

If you are able to walk away with something from my experiences, even the negative ones, or are able to listen to some honest advice about preparing for something, then I did my job today. I will be eternally grateful if one thing I have to say sticks with you for tomorrow, or the rest of your life. I am trying my best to spearhead the expedition through college and make it easier on you, so if I am able to do that, you just made me the happiest person in the world!

Again, I am looking forward to sharing this experience with you, and we will try our best to prepare you for college and the real world!

Love always,
Haley

CHAPTER 1

WHILE YOU'RE STILL IN HIGH SCHOOL

You may be asking yourself why this book has a high school section when it is being touted as a college freshman's survival guide. Most of the stepping-stones to becoming a college freshman and beginning to think about higher education begin in high school.

Most of the important highlights of high school and the preparation for college begin during the junior year of high school. My junior year of high school was filled with momentous events for my future, including taking standardized tests, meeting with a college advisor for the first time, deciding where I might want to go to school, and thinking about what I would write on a college essay to stand out from other students from all over the country applying to the same schools as I was. My senior year had prom, graduation, acceptances, and the final decision of where I would spend my next four years. The end of high school is truly special and important for the future!

Thinking about the rest of your life

By your junior year of high school, it is important to have some sort of idea about your future and continuing your education.

This does not necessarily mean you have to know exactly what you want to do, but it means you need to begin considering your options. Some of these options include going to a university, community college, trade or vocational school, entering special programs for those with disabilities, or getting a job. The majority of this book focuses on going to a four-year university, but I will touch on your other options if you are considering those.

I want it to be clear that some of the decisions you will make in high school will follow you the rest of your life. The goal is to keep as many options open as you possibly can. If your grades are not as high as they should be, you will be closing doors and having fewer options because your dream school may want certain grade point averages (GPAs) or grades for acceptances. While you may not be sure what you want to do just yet, have ideas of what interests you and explore, and keep your grades high so you do have options available to you when you are applying to colleges and making decisions on where to go after high school.

College fairs

If you are considering a four-year college and are not sure where to begin your search, attend a school or local college fair. My high school held a college fair, and so did my county. At a college fair, representatives from many colleges and universities across the country (and sometimes even abroad) set up a table with brochures and allow you to ask questions and pick up materials so you can learn more on your own after the fair. The representatives are usually admissions officers who read applications and make decisions. When speaking to the representatives, be courteous and polite, and don't be afraid to ask questions!

Often at college fairs I have been asked to sign up for email and mailing lists. If you are asked to sign up and have any interest whatsoever in the college, sign up! It shows the representative that you are interested, and there is always the chance that the representative will remember you if he or she is reading your application sometime.

If you know you are considering specific colleges and they are not at a college fair, sometimes the college will host a nighttime event at a hotel in your area. These events usually have alumni representatives and allow your entire family to attend with you. They are similar to the college fair in which you can ask questions, but are only for one specific college. Do not go to these meet-ups unless you are serious about the school or really want more information.

College counseling and advisors

Halfway through my junior year of high school, I was assigned a college counselor to meet with regularly and review the application process and prospective options with. My counselor was very friendly and kind, but did not often realize the needs I had with my autism. My private high school dealt with almost all neurotypical kids who were expected to go to top universities in the United States, and that wasn't something I wanted to do. I knew with my autism I had limitations. By my junior year, I knew there was no way I would be able to attend a university that was only accessible to me by plane. I made the first of many decisions with my counselor (with his initial disapproval) to stay in the state of Florida because I knew everything was accessible by car, and that if I wanted to go home, I could.

Outside of listing prospective options, my college counselor also served as an advisor for planning my senior year coursework. We picked which classes would look best on a transcript, given I was not leaving my home state (he recommended I take a fourth year of foreign language), while making sure I had time to work on my applications, essays, artwork, and other interests.

The best advice I got through the college advising process was having a third opinion to look over my applications and essays. I would read my essays and think they were up to par with what admissions officers were looking for, and my parents liked my essays, but I learned that wasn't all that admissions officers wanted to see. My advisor read and revised every draft of the college essays which I submitted, until they were perfectly crafted stories and were ready to be submitted to the six different schools I ended up applying to.

However, there are also private counseling services that may better suit your needs than the ones provided at school. My school's college advisors and counselors had never dealt with people in my situation. It is important to realize your strengths, limitations, and options as a person with autism or special needs. There are private counselors that specifically work with students with differences in order to find programs and universities that will best accommodate their needs. It might be an expensive option, but it could serve as a valuable opinion to help prepare for the future, keeping in mind the challenges you are facing.

Working with college advisors and counselors is a valuable experience during the application process, but when it comes to weighing in your options, it is important to be realistic, and the entire college decision process is mainly a series of decisions. Take it one step at a time—my first decision was to stay locally in state so I could continue to receive support from home and have the option to come home. I also was not sure how I felt about living away at the time, so being able to stay somewhat locally gave me the option to either live at home or live in a more traditional dormitory setting.

Finances

Given today's economic issues around the globe, it would be a shame for me to avoid talking briefly about finances and college. If you keep up with current events, you have probably heard about student loans and student debt many times. It is especially important to consider finances with students with ASDs because their futures are sometimes uncertain. Their dropout rates are higher than those of neurotypical students, and it is more important than ever to plan for the future with ASDs.

Basically, plan accordingly. If you are planning on going to professional or graduate school, try to plan how you will pay for that before worrying about accumulating massive amounts of debt for an undergraduate education. Think smartly when it comes to financing your college career for a variety of reasons!

I am by no means a finance expert, which is why I don't have much advice to give you other than to plan ahead and make a decision as a family. You never know what the future may bring, and an expensive, private undergraduate education may not be worth the price of admission.

Special programs/schools for those with Autism Spectrum Disorders/online options

If you do not feel ready for college or aren't able to go to college, there are special options for those with ASDs. There are special schools exclusively for those with ASDs, usually spearheaded by charitable organizations. These types of programs have a larger focus on vocational training than preparation for a degree or graduate program, so it is more of an option if college is not part of your future plan!

If you want to go to college but do not yet feel ready, there are also preparation programs out there for students with differences such as the College Internship Program (CIP). CIPs are hosted on college campuses around the United States, and prepare students to go to college by simulating independent living, job training, and other situations with lots of support. Whether you think you are ready or not for college is a personal and family decision, and if you feel uncomfortable with living away from home there are also local options such as community colleges, a large university close to home that you could commute to, or distance learning.

There are also programs for students with learning differences and ASDs at regular universities. Do your research and find colleges that have support and programs in order to help those with learning disabilities succeed and plan ahead towards their degrees and employment. When I first spoke at the Autism Society of America conference in 2008, Marshall University in West Virginia was beginning an Asperger Syndrome (AS) mentoring program, where an autistic student would be given an older student mentor to help them and support them during the college years. It takes some more research and funds since these programs are usually at private colleges, but they could be beneficial as well. Many other colleges are following this model, so research which colleges are "autism friendly" so you can get the support you need to succeed.

I also want to share that by the time this book is in your hands, online college degrees through distance learning will be a real option. My college already began implementing programs where you never had to physically attend a class. You could complete your entire degree from your bedroom in your parents' house, and then pretty much every single worry you have about going to a real college is negated. With an online degree, you must complete your coursework on time, follow the rules, and keep a schedule. I would look into this if you want to pursue a college degree and either don't have the time, if you don't feel ready but want to get started, or if the college experiences of living away, socializing, and learning to be fully independent are not important to you yet.

Standardized tests and college entrance exams

If you are going to college, the first important step to prepare for college applications are standardized tests. American colleges and universities accept either the SAT, the ACT, or both. The SAT is comprised of math sections and English sections as well as an essay portion and is scored out of 2400. The ACT is comprised of reading, English, math, science, and an essay section and is scored out of 36. Most students will do better on one test than the other, and it's up to you to find out which test that is. Personally, I found the ACT easier because I found the English section was more common sense and grammar, while the SAT English section was more vocabulary oriented. Other countries have college entrance exams with similar information on them pertaining to language skills, mathematics, and writing.

In order to prepare for these tests, most kids buy preparation books online and complete practice tests. Practice test results will tell you which is "your test." If your high school offers a preparation class, take it. Some kids also have private tutors in order to help them score higher and focus on their weak points, which are revealed through practice tests. I had a private tutor for the math sections and learned strategies for taking the tests, such as how to guess and how the questions were ordered by level of difficulty. Math was not my strong suit when I took my standardized tests. Make sure you have a background in geometry and algebra before beginning college entrance exam prep; if not, spend extra time teaching and reviewing these subjects to yourself.

Before test day, make sure you are registered through the testing websites at a specified test center. If you want accommodations such as extra time to take the test, make sure you register for that as well. Sometimes, it is a good idea to take the test at a test site that is a different school than the one you go to. You will be less likely to see people you know and get distracted. Most tests are early in the morning, so in order to begin your test taking properly, get a good night's sleep the night before and wear comfortable clothes to the test site. Pack a sweater as well in case the test room is cold. You will need to bring your ID (preferably a driver's license or learning permit), testing registration information, an approved calculator, and lots of number-two pencils with you. If you are easily distracted, ask your proctor if you could sit in the front of the room before the test starts because you are less likely to notice other people and look at them while you work.

When you take the test, it is important not to be nervous and to try your best. Certain tests penalize for guessing, so if you do not feel as if you know an answer, skip the question and come back to it later. I would usually circle this question's number on the answer sheet very lightly or in the test booklet so I knew to come back to it. If you still do not know the answer and would be penalized for guessing, leave it blank, as no points are deducted for unanswered questions. Other tests do not penalize for guessing, so if you can narrow the choices down, it is in your best interest to guess. You will get your scores in the mail several weeks later and you will know if you have to retake the test based on your scores and what you are aiming for. Check the average scores online for the colleges and universities you would like to apply to.

I took the SAT once and the ACT twice. If you are unhappy with your scores even after the spring of your junior year, you can take them in the summer, or right at the start of your senior year in September and October, but if a college application is due before November 1, prepare to rush to get those scores sent out! I probably should have taken the ACT one more time, which I was advised to, but I was pretty satisfied with how I did and I really did not want to sit through another five hours of testing on a Saturday by September of my senior year. I just wanted to be done with everything, and my score was above the minimum for almost every school in the state of Florida anyway, so I didn't really see the point of taking standardized tests one final time.

Applications, essays, and recommendations

After taking the SATs and deciding on your options, it is time to start writing the applications! Each school's application process is a little bit different, and the deadlines are all different based on the type of application you file.

Almost all applications can be submitted online. I only sent one hard-copy application. The first step is to register for the Common Application (www.commonapp.org). Many schools in the United States and several in Europe use the Common Application, and you can pretty much fill out the same vital information about yourself once to use on multiple applications. See which of the schools you are applying to use the Common Application, and this determines how many schools will be getting the same information except for the supplemental sections—you even can submit the same personal essay to all these different schools. I applied to six colleges, and two of them used the Common Application, so that was one less application I had to fill out.

All applications make you indicate a type of decision that you want your application to fall under, based on the school's different acceptance policies: Early Decision (ED), Early Action (EA), Regular Decision (RD), and Rolling Decision. Each of these policies has different terms of agreement upon acceptance. ED is a type of decision that you can only put down for one college (unless they let you do ED1 and ED2, in which case you can put two different schools for early decision). ED notifies you of your acceptance, denial, or deferral as early as mid-December. However, if you are accepted ED, that means you put the school down as your first choice and that is where you will be attending in the fall. It is difficult to get out of a binding ED agreement, so be aware of what you are doing if you choose to apply ED. EA is unbinding, but allows you to find out your decision early (typically in February, as opposed to April 1). Sometimes, you can only choose this option for one school through single choice EA. RD is when you find out on April 1, or in rare circumstances, earlier. Rolling Decision is based on when your application is submitted, and you will find out within several weeks. Rolling Decision is great for the confidence boost of an early acceptance if you are proactive about your applications—I finished my first few Rolling Decision applications at the end of September of my senior year, and had acceptances by Halloween, so unlike most high school seniors, I had the peace of mind of knowing I was accepted somewhere.

Recommendations

Most applications also require you secure recommendations from teachers you had throughout high school. Recommendations serve to tell the college about what type of student and person you are. In most cases it is best to ask at least two teachers to write on your behalf, and you typically ask near the end of your junior year if a teacher would be willing to write a recommendation for you. When choosing teachers to write you recommendations, try to ask the ones who seem to know you best both inside and out of class. Maybe there's one teacher from freshman year whose class you didn't do amazingly in, but she saw your willingness to learn and helped you out after school. That is the teacher you would approach about writing your recommendation. You will most likely never get to see the recommendations, so it is up to you to trust in them and either ask your advisor or follow up yourself several weeks later to find out if the recommendation has been submitted to the college advising office or as part of the application for a specific college already.

The essay

The most universal part of an application, regardless of decision type or means by which it is sent, is the essay. The essay is your chance to stand out and show a college admissions committee who you are outside of test scores, a list of activities, and grades. The major goal of the typical college essay is usually to tell a story about yourself or write about an experience, while remaining as memorable as possible. Sometimes, telling the story of a special interest of yours may be a good idea—one of the best essays that our advisors shared with us was about a boy's stamp collecting hobby. However, the biggest challenge of these essays, other than being memorable, is the fact that you do not get a lot of space to write. The typical college essay usually hovers at around 500–600 words, which is about a page. It really isn't a lot of room to express yourself, so it is also your job to make the most out of what you are given. You want to start your essay with something interesting to grab your reader's attention, and from there tell your story. If you need help writing your essay, there are lots of great resources online and as an example, I have decided to share my Common Application essay with you all:

> Here I was, fresh off the red carpet and staring directly at former President Clinton. I stood up on my chair at Cipriani Wall Street just to catch a glimpse of the former President while he was onstage. I was moments away from Dan Marino introducing me as the Samsung Teen Hero honoree. I was even several more moments away from delivering an

acceptance speech to the crowd of **800**. All I could think to myself was "how am I here right now?"

I was diagnosed with high-functioning autism at the age of three. It was never really something I planned to "come out" with to my friends, my peers, or even the general public. Simply put, my passion for helping others was purely accidental. I knew I had autism since the age of nine, but I didn't see the need to make it public knowledge. My thoughts were along the lines of "Why stick a label on me? I'm not a can of Campbell's Soup."

At the end of my freshman year of high school, I joined forces with a local autism organization to raise money through my artwork at an event. To spread the word, I handed my English teacher an invitation. He was so thrilled with me that I had to give a presentation to my classmates on what I was doing—the catch was my teacher forgot to tell me I had to talk about autism until I was halfway through. Go figure that's how I was "outed" to my school community. Yet after I told my class about my life with autism, I felt completely inspired. Very few of them knew anything at all about autism, or had a family member with the neurological disorder and therefore, they asked me a lot of questions.

From that day on, I made sure I could give as many talks as possible. Not many people viewed a disability as a positive asset like I did, and so many people in my own community were unaware of what autism was or how it affects somebody with it. When I was on CNN Newsroom, the video clips online were titled with my message on how I viewed my disability as an undeniable strength. That night alone, I received over **150** personal emails, thanking me for bravely sharing my story and "giving hope," and most importantly, allowing people to see autism in a different light, rather than the "doom and gloom" prognoses given to parents of newly diagnosed children.

"And here I am." Because of my public speaking and fundraising to benefit the autism cause, Samsung International chose me as their Teen Hero Honoree. I want to play an important role in shaping the future on how the world views people with autism. It is my goal and dream to help raise awareness and funding to support others with this disorder so that they can acwhieve their dreams. While onstage at Cipriani, I made sure everyone knew they had the power to make a difference. I also made a personal promise to myself that I would continue to change the perception of autism and forever be an artist, author and an advocate.

My essay served to tell a story of a life-changing event and a call to leadership. I tried to be as memorable as possible by mentioning the famous people I met, and telling the story of my autism and success with it was not typical. Like I said, this was about telling a story more than it was about writing a good essay.

Sometimes, you will be asked for additional essays or alternative essays on an application. With these atypical essays, you are most likely going to be prompted to answer specific questions about a single college, such as why you want to attend. If you have to write these types of essays, my best advice to you is to sound clear, concise, and mature. Be honest, and take care to make sure all the information is right. Putting information for the wrong college on a college-specific essay is a surefire way to get denied come decision time, since it represents a lack of interest and knowledge about the subject you wrote about.

Visiting campuses and pretending to investigate

While you are applying to college or right before you apply, you and your family may feel it is necessary to visit the college campus. Most students go on campus tours during their junior years and while their applications are still pending, but in other cases, visiting a college campus could help your case for an application since it once again demonstrates interest in the college, and you will most likely meet with someone in admissions. The admissions officer will be introduced to you and your family, and either they or a student ambassador will give you a tour of the campus if the tours are run through admissions. If the tours are not run through the admissions office, it will be more like my university where a student group under a different department runs the tours (in our case, the student alumni association). The student ambassador is a current student who is either a volunteer or paid employee, who gives you a tour of the campus and honestly points out places of interest to students. The student-led tour is usually much more informative for a prospective student since it is less about showing you the beauty of the campus, and more about the realistic experience that a student has.

Before you go on tour, think of a few things about college that concern you and make a mental list of questions to ask. My first area of concern was food-related because I am a very picky eater, and would hate not to know what to eat while on campus. I would think of questions related to food to ask a student tour guide, or if you're not with a student guide, go up to random students and ask these types of questions in a much more general way (is the dining hall food good?). My food questions were whether the food was good and if they offered pizza and/or chicken nuggets. Often, the guides would laugh or be confused, but I knew this was an important question to ask given my limited food choices. Your family may also have questions for this list of their own, such as what types of support and services are available for students with autism, etc. You could also ask about living arrangements and roommates if you prefer your own space, since often campuses have single rooms available or accommodations for students with special needs. Simply put, be prepared to ask questions while on tour!

While you're looking at schools, it is also important to observe the student body. See what people look like, if they are talking to each other, and strangely enough, what they are wearing. This is the kind of important information that will help you if this is the college you end up attending. For instance, at my college, a lot of girls wear cowboy boots as a fashion trend. However, my campus tour was on a Saturday morning and I did not see many students on campus (a lot of students sleep late on the weekends, simply because they can). On other campuses I noticed fashion trends, types of backpacks everyone had, etc. This information will help you gauge if the students seem friendly, what's popular, and help you acclimatize to campus faster.

My next piece of advice to you is to try to get as full a tour as possible. Sometimes, admissions officers and student ambassadors don't get to show you everything you may want to see. Often, students want to see dorm rooms and dining halls, and rarely get to see dorm rooms. It is okay to ask to see a dorm room, since often there are sample rooms they have available to show prospective students. If there are no model rooms, on some occasions the tour guides will allow you to see their own personal rooms if their roommate is okay with it. Do not judge or comment if the room is not to your taste or is disorganized. Observe and see what types of things they have, how their interactions with their roommates are, and other things rather than the décor or lack of organization.

If you did not get to see everything you want on a tour but were admitted to the school, many colleges have a "preview day" for accepted high school seniors in which they get to shadow a current student for the day. On these preview days, students get to eat in the dining halls (a great thing, especially if you have food issues), visit their host's dorm rooms, and even go to class. On preview days, your decision should be clearer as you interact with current students and live the life of a college student for the day.

Picking the right college

After all your efforts on your applications and essays, and seeking guidance, the time has come when your acceptance letters and emails are showing up. Congratulations! Now is the hard part: choosing which of these fine institutions you want to attend in the fall (or spring or summer, depending on which term you were admitted for). To help you narrow it down, here are some points you should consider.

If you have not taken a tour of the schools you were admitted to, now is the time you should be touring. Since you're an admitted student, you aren't looking at colleges unrealistically and can have a much clearer view of things. Could you picture yourself as a student here? Do the people seem friendly? There are lots of factors to consider, and in this section I'm going to start listing some good things for you to consider in your choice.

How far away from home are you?

If you are really far away from home, you might need to take an airplane to get to your college, or take a long-distance bus line. You and your family will also need to factor in these costs of transportation. Being far away from home also limits how often you will come home. Typically, students whose families live far away only go home at Thanksgiving, Christmas, Spring Break and summertime. If you go to school very close to home, you could commute and live at home, or still live away and come home often. It is up to you and your comfort level as well as your family to decide how far you ideally would like to be. If you live away from home, you may also have a roommate in a dorm room or an apartment, depending on where you are.

By car, I am four hours away from home. I come home anywhere from every two to six weeks, depending on my mood and if I feel I need to get away from my college town and want a break, or just simple things like a haircut, good shopping, or more time with my family. I am able to get home by taking a bus across the state and it takes five hours each way and is very reliable and inexpensive. Coming home is a breeze, and if my parents ever wanted to visit (which I highly advise against since coming home is much more exciting, but we will cover that later in this book!), they still could. It is the perfect distance that I still live away but if I ever needed something or was sick, I could still visit and all packages come within two days as well.

How big a school do you want to be at?

At first, I thought I wanted to be at a small liberal arts college where my professors would know me, everyone knew everyone, and things would be great. However, every little school I toured had little things I wished were there and weren't. I found there weren't enough diverse opportunities, and I was scared that in some of these little colleges (the smallest I was accepted to had 300 students), it would be much harder to make friends with similar interests because there was such a limited group of people. When I toured my current college, I loved it. I loved how spirited and alive it felt with all 50,000 combined undergraduate and graduate students. It was springtime and I could already imagine how alive the football stadium would be when fall came. However, the excitement and community my school embodies does not mean it does not have its problems, too. I do not personally know any of my professors, and it is still hard to meet people since there is so much to get involved with or do that it is easy to get lost along the way.

Do you have an idea of what you want to do after college?

I know that knowing what you want to do at 16–18 years old is very scary and very tentative. I've changed my mind more times than I could count. However, if you have a general idea of what might interest you (for instance, you love math), look at the schools based on what programs they offer. If the program in your ideal field of study is very strong, that is a huge factor to consider. My school has a very strong journalism department, so anyone in my state who considers going into television or any news-related field usually goes to my college because of the strong placement into jobs and the background they will gain in the field. If you think you will change your mind (which 68 percent of college students do within the first two years according to our university advising website), choose a school that caters to your wide array of interests or will let you explore new things that you may have never found yourself interested in before. You want the freedom to learn more, since later in life you might never have the time to learn on your own, even if it's more of a "for fun" thing. I took a course on eating disorders last semester because I thought it was interesting. I never thought I would get to do that.

What are the disability-related support systems like?

This might matter to your family more than it matters to you, especially if you think you are perfectly capable of living on your own and taking care of yourself. However, although you may think that and believe it, it never hurts to have a place on campus with adults you can trust and who will understand you and your challenges. If you need extra test time, accommodations to meet with your teacher, or a special note-taker in your class, the disability center or staff can usually help you in arranging such things. My university's disability center has been nothing but kind to me, and they helped me get better housing arrangements by pointing me to the right people in housing, and they also had a weekly support group for students with AS. I am not an active member of the support group, but I went once just to see what it was all about and I will share more about that experience later.

What about challenges specific to me?

You might also want to consider challenges that are specific to you when picking the right college, whether it be a need for personal space, food, or something completely random that I might not be able to address.

My biggest specific challenge was food, since I pretty much eat pizza, chicken nuggets, desserts, and lots of breakfast food (cereal, pancakes, and waffles). I was looking for a campus that would accommodate my issues without me formalizing a request with the dining hall. My university is a life-saver in this department because not only does one of the two dining halls have pizza every single night, but they also have fast food chain restaurants on campus, so I can get whatever I want. I also love that we have some chains on campus that I don't have back home, so it was a real treat for the first couple weeks while at school.

Grades

Although we just had a conversation about picking the right college and you're probably a very bored high school senior anticipating graduation at this point, it is still important not to let your grades fall. All offers of admissions are tentative, which means if you are suddenly failing everything because you decided to slack off in the homestretch, the college could rescind (take back) their admission to you. Do not let anything fall more than a plus or minus if your grades are falling. More than a full letter grade is an issue. High school is not over until the day you receive your diploma, so make sure to keep up the good work and don't fail anything or accumulate a bunch of random absences.

Prom

Prom might not be something that interests you if you're a student on the spectrum. It surely didn't interest me during my junior or senior year. In recent times, prom is more about the way a girl is asked than anything else. "Prom proposals" are elaborate ways that guys ask girls, whether through a bunch of balloons on their lockers, serenading them, making corny signs, you name it. You would think it looks like a marriage proposal, hence the widely accepted term "promposal." Most girls honestly want to go to shop for and wear a nice dress, socialize and go to after-parties. Boys usually go for the socializing and the after-parties. Prom after-parties are usually stocked up with liquor and lots of drunken sex, so I would not advise going.

Despite my feelings about prom, I did end up going to my senior prom. I've told my prom story hundreds of times to close family friends and people in college because we all think it's funny in hindsight. My date was a friend of mine who went to my high school and was currently home from college for the summer. He wanted to go since he didn't go to his own prom, and we said we would go. I had a nice black dress, picked out the boutonnière and corsage, the whole deal. I wanted it right since it would be the first and last time I would go to prom.

My high school was lame and held it in the gymnasium instead of a nice hotel like most other proms, so there was no good food or anything. I saw all my peers who I didn't really enjoy spending time with and felt mentally done with after four years, since I couldn't wait for college orientation two weeks later. We left prom after about an hour and a half and a few dances, and decided to go out to dinner to a nice restaurant to compensate for how boring prom was. However, when the check came, my date did not have money to pay so I had to pay for both of us! Prom becomes a rite of passage that helps start conversations in college since everyone has a story about who their date was, the venue, or a party.

That's pretty much what prom is before you go to college. It's one last hurrah with all your high school friends (or lack thereof), and a story you will tell one day to make people laugh. It's also a great excuse for your parents to take tons of pictures of you in formalwear.

Graduation

Graduation is one of the most exciting times in a high schooler's life despite the amount of family drama that goes down before graduation, including who is invited, who isn't, will there be a party, what kind of gifts do you want. It is the final hurrah and means you made it, and your family is so proud of you as you receive your diploma and move onto the next adventure in your life.

Graduation was emotional for my family. We were told when I was first diagnosed with autism that we had so much to fear, and that day was the day it was all proven wrong. I was headed to the best school in the entire state of Florida. I had my roommate waiting to greet me with open arms in August. We made it through so much, and this was the day we were waiting for. I graduated with honors and awards for national community service recognition. My mom cried even though she found our ceremony to be tacky. We celebrated later, and had lots of fun celebrating the beginning of a new era.

What about my friends?

If you were like me and had very few, if any, friends in high school, you don't have too much to worry about. Once you go to college, you will rarely see anyone you went to high school with, even if they go to the same college with you. I had 20 kids from my high school go to the same school as I did and I saw maybe four of them throughout the course of a year. Use college as a chance to start afresh, especially if you were bullied in high school. You may never see those bullies again!

I have not seen any of my high school friends since the day we graduated. We barely even stay in touch. Sometimes, if I am feeling sentimental, I send them a Facebook message once or twice per semester to see how they are, or ask when they are coming home. Like me, you may find that some of your friendships get reduced to Facebook friends, with the exception of family friends or best friends since birth. It's worth making an effort to stay in touch with close high school friends and to see them at vacation times if they don't go to your college.

If you do have friends that are starting at the same college as you, it could be a big support and may help you to feel less lonely. Sometimes, though, it helps not to rely too much on your high school friends when starting your new adventure so you are more open-minded to meeting new people. Also don't be surprised if you start to see less of your old friends as they begin to meet new people too.

CHAPTER 2

GETTING READY FOR COLLEGE

I remember my mother came home with bed linens and other household items during the summer of my senior year at school, and I just felt bewildered. We weren't moving as a family, and I wasn't repainting and redoing my bedroom at home, so why did I need all of this brand new stuff? As my senior year went on and I was filling out applications, requesting transcripts to be sent, and sending official test results, my mom was buying anything and everything a girl could ever want (or need): lots and lots of clothes, decorations, towels, shower shoes and caddies, clocks, band-aids, mattress pads, and so much more. I remember the room where we kept all of this, "Haley's college dorm room," was overflowing, to the point where I was scared to enter the room. I was stressed out by the idea of not living at home months later, and I really didn't seem to take an interest in the continuous shopping extravaganza.

In hindsight, though, I really admire my mother's proactive agenda in regards to setting up my future residence, although at the time we had no idea where it would be, if I would have to share a room, or anything. It made moving in that much less stressful, and made packing a breeze the summer before I moved into my dorm room. It made a *lot* of sense to buy things before we knew we even needed them and before everyone else and their mothers would be buying the same things! I planned on living in a dorm once again for my sophomore year, so when I brought everything home for the summer, we packed it up to go back to school just like the year before—except I chose to "thin out the herd" and take less, since I knew what was and wasn't important and how much storage space I had.

Basically, if you aren't one for anecdotes, or don't have time or a vested interest in reading my personal opinions or stories on getting ready for college, walk away with this one key point: *be proactive. Start getting ready early.*

Housing arrangements

Now that you know where you are going, you may or may not have already made housing arrangements. Most likely you will be living in a dorm with a roommate. I was very afraid to live with a roommate because of my autism, and my mom called the disability office a few months prior to orientation and they put me in touch with people in housing. Housing offered me a single room, and I declined because I wanted the typical college experience of living with a roommate. I told them I wanted to live with an upperclassman because I thought it would be helpful to have a "big sister" type to help acclimatize me and answer any questions I would have. We decided as a group that the campus honors dorm was the best place for me because of its quiet atmosphere and more private living arrangements (four girls to a suite, two bedrooms, one bathroom). I got to meet and socialize with three different girls a year older than me who lived in the honors dorms and needed a roommate for the upcoming year. I really enjoyed talking to all of them. One of them I felt was very similar to me, but she was quiet. I wanted to live with someone more outgoing so I would get to meet more people and come out of my comfort zone, so I chose the most outgoing one. Unfortunately, what I saw that day was not what I ended up with and we had several disagreements and assorted roommate issues, and now I have a single room all to myself. However, having this conversation with housing got me in touch with the right people and helped ease my fears at the time, and when I did want a single room, I was able to get one. It is okay if your parents call the first time because you are still in high school and are not expected to handle everything on your own yet.

If you are leaving it to chance and going with a random roommate, that is okay! I know some people who met their best friends through random roommates, and others who hated their random roommates. It is in your best interest to reach out to your roommate when you get their contact information and begin your relationship! It is okay if you don't feel like you met your new best friend. With roommates, they need to be respectful and easy to get along with and live with. You don't have to be a good friend to be a good roommate!

Dorm life is the most common arrangement that incoming college freshmen choose. Dorms usually have very little privacy, are loud, social, and community-oriented. You will probably share a bathroom with multiple people so you might not get privacy when you brush your teeth, and gossip is rampant. Most of the bedrooms have two or three people living in them, and in very rare instances there are single rooms for one person only. Other dorms have four-person setups, where there are four single bedrooms that share a kitchen and a sitting area. Those are typically less social than a building consisting of singles, doubles, and triples. Instead of having a parent or a management group looking after the building, each floor has a Resident Assistant (RA). An RA is an older student who is paid to keep the residence hall rules enforced, be a good listener, mentor, and resolve conflicts.

If dorm life might not be for you because of the community feeling and the lack of privacy, an apartment or small house may be better for you. If your college is in a traditional college town, there are usually student apartments that aren't quite like regular apartments. Student apartments are typically shared with roommates, but you aren't living in as closed quarters as in a dorm. Student apartments allow each person to have their own bedroom and bathroom that can be locked (which has lots of privacy), and the roommates share common spaces like the kitchen, living room, and often a washing machine and a dryer. Regular apartments may have multiple bedrooms but you might be sharing a bathroom. When renting an apartment or a house, make sure your parents are present and that you go over all the terms of the lease, understand the costs and fees involved, and check everything is okay when you move into the unit so you are not charged for damages you never created. However, if you are living in an apartment or a house, you will also be further away from campus and still have roommates, even though you are not sharing bedroom space like you would in an average dorm room.

If you choose to be a commuter student and go to a local college, you might be living at home. Living at home is still a valuable experience since your parents may allow you to become more independent and rely on taking yourself places and keeping your own schedule. However, living at home is also more of a challenge, since you might feel removed from experiences such as sharing space with strangers, having a roommate, and being extra close to campus so going to meetings or social gatherings is not as much of an issue.

After your first year there are also other special living arrangements available. If you are a member of a social fraternity or a sorority, you might be allowed to live inside the chapter's house instead of a dorm or an apartment. You should not be assuming you will get to live in one of these houses when you are first planning on moving, so see if this is something that interests you about halfway through your first year if it is what you want for the future.

Dorm room essentials

As I discussed in the opening portion of this chapter, packing for my dorm room was a long ordeal because we began buying things to place in my room almost a year in advance. Packing for your dorm room is one of the most exciting and stressful times as you begin to realize that college is in the immediate future.

First off, let's start with what you are prohibited from bringing into dorms since many dorms and residence halls have a very similar list of no-nos. Anything that could jeopardize your safety or the safety of the other residents is never allowed. Candles and incense are some of the things you shouldn't even consider bringing, as they are fire hazards and burning down your building shouldn't be an option. The same goes for weapons (large knives, guns, etc.) and drug paraphernalia. If you want a pet, you should see what your building's rules are regarding pets (my residence hall allowed smaller animals if you registered them, such as rabbits, lizards, guinea pigs, fish, and hamsters). They usually won't let you have a dog or cat, but if you have a service animal or live elsewhere, you might be able to get around this.

The most obvious thing to bring into the dorm should be a bed set. A nice comforter, sheets, blankets, pillows, and pillowcases are necessities. Dorm mattresses are typically very firm and very uncomfortable, so a mattress pad helps to make it softer and more durable. I also had a bed bug protector on my mattress because I wasn't sure who lived there before me, and what types of critters may be around the corner. If your bedding allows for matching decorations, throw pillows are a homey touch (but they may end up on the floor a lot, especially if your bed is your main workspace). If you want a stuffed animal, or other things like that, it is fine too. When you are making your bed, try to raise it a little bit higher than you normally would if you are able to because by elevating the bed, you are creating extra storage space, which is very important!

The next big thing you should bring is storage. Space is limited in dorm rooms, and often storage containers help make the most out of your space. I had collapsible storage boxes I kept under the bed. That way, if the box was empty or I had too many boxes, I could fold them up and have them take up minimal room. I labeled my boxes as the "pharmacy box," "house box," "clothes box," and "products box." My "pharmacy box" contained first-aid items and common over-the-counter medications. I had band-aids, rubbing alcohol, cold and allergy medications, ibuprofen, Icy

Hot packs, and other essentials in the event that I got sick. My "house box" contained silverware, plates, cups, laundry detergent pods, Command Strips, ink for my printer, and other random items that would normally be found in the house. My "clothes box" contained extra items I didn't have room for in the closet or drawers, such as socks and workout clothes. My "products box" held mainly bathroom essentials and this box will probably be of most use to you, especially if you have a community bathroom setting and do not have your own bathroom to store things in. That box had cleaners, extra shampoo, makeup, Q-tips, shaving cream, toothpaste, toothbrushes, disposable razors, small hand towels, a bowl to keep my retainers in when they were being cleaned, dental cleaner tablets, floss, etc. It was easier to pack these boxes before so everything took up less space. If your closet space is limited (which it probably will be), Space Bags are also a good idea. These are the bags that you pack up with folded items and then blow dry or vacuum out the air so everything takes up less space. Thin hangers are also a good idea since they allow you to hang extra clothes in the closet too.

Since you are most likely sharing a bathroom, in order to keep your stuff separate and in your room to avoid theft, buy a shower caddy. Inside of your shower caddy should be shampoo, conditioner, body wash, shaving cream, a razor, a shower cap, and shower shoes. Towels are also important to have! If you're a girl, you might want to see how the community bathrooms look before bringing in all your hair drying and straightening products because you might end up doing it in your dorm room if your roommate isn't home or doesn't care.

Next is your desk area. Your desk area is typically where you are going to spend most of your working time. For this, you're going to want a good lamp that isn't a fire hazard. I ended up getting a lamp from Ikea. It was under $20, and was small and powerful. It also bent so I was able to adjust where the light would shine. If you want a decorative lamp, keep it by your bed. With your desk, you are going to want to pack basic office supplies if you do not buy them while in your college town. Pencils, pens, notebooks, highlighters, a basic color pencil set, folders, binders, tape, and index cards could all be stored in a drawer in your desk, and will always come in handy once the school year begins. With your desk, you are also going to want to bring your laptop computer, its charger and a printer (computer buying and setup will be covered shortly with other technology products) since it will primarily be set up in the center of your desk.

If you do not plan on relying on a meal plan your entire year, get a refrigerator! Even though dorms typically have a common kitchen area for cooking, they rarely have refrigerators for the entire floor to use, and if they do, other residents will likely eat your food. Smaller appliances are best since they can still be carried up the stairs if your building does not have an elevator and you most likely will not be sharing with your roommate unless you two previously discussed that. In your fridge should be healthy snacks or cold drinks—things you might need or want while studying, or when the dining halls are closed. If you are relying on providing meals for yourself, stock your fridge with important ingredients and foods to cook for yourself such as meat, yogurt, fruit, and other common food products you see at home. A microwave may also be a good thing to have. Dorm kitchens often have microwaves, but if you don't like sharing then I think you should get your own. If you are cooking for yourself, choose easy to make things since most appliances, like ovens, are shared between entire floors and are not always the most reliable or accessible. If a fridge and a microwave are not enough for you when providing for yourself, there are also other small appliances such as toaster ovens and blenders you could get. However, once again: beware of the space issue since there is never enough room in a dorm (especially if you have a roommate)! If you know your dorm's mailing address, I recommend you order the fridge and microwave online via a site like Amazon so you do not have to fit it into your car, or on an airplane. You also won't have to lift it more times than needed. If Amazon is not an option, buy the fridge while in your college town, at a Wal-Mart or something, so the bulky appliance only has to travel a few miles instead of far away.

Keep in mind that the dorm room is going to most likely be your home for the next year, so do not feel afraid to personalize it in mostly quick ways that allow you to remove everything by the end of the spring semester! If you are planning on hanging anything on the walls, Command Strips are lifesavers. You basically just peel off the tape and stick them to the wall, and they adhere to posters/décor or serve as hooks for towels and artwork. If you plan on hanging photos or making a photo collage to remember everyone and things back home, buy a corkboard and thumbtacks to put the photos on, and then hang the board with a Command Strip. Bring anything you want from home to make your room feel special and like a home away from home. I had posters of my artwork hanging all over the room to keep it colorful; I had little trinkets on my desk. Some of you may also want to bring a plant to make it feel homey—my advice is, buy a fake plant because you don't have to water it and the minute you get bugs from a real plant, you and/or your roommate will freak out.

Because your room is a miniature home, you will also need to take care of it and do a lot of maintenance on your space and belongings. You are also responsible for keeping the room clean. Depending on the type of flooring you have, you will rely on certain tools more than others. My room had carpeting so I relied very heavily on the vacuums that were available for rent downstairs. Looking back at my freshman year, I wish I packed a smaller vacuum so I wouldn't have to bring a huge commercial vacuum back and forth up two flights of stairs. For the future, I bought a Dirt Devil that I can plug in and move portably with ease. I also had cleaning supplies to clean the mirror and windows. Bring some air fresheners or extra cologne or perfume to get rid of bad smells and make the room smell good as well. You are also going to want to keep your belongings clean. Bring a duster. If you live in an old building or a building that is known to have bug problems (which sadly could happen before you even move in), bring a can of aerosol or a common bug killer so you can sleep at night without fear. The most important belongings you are going to want to keep clean are your clothes and bedding, so bringing laundry supplies such as detergent, a hamper for dirty clothes, and laundry bags is important. I personally recommend laundry detergent pods, since you don't have to pour anything and they are easy to transport to the laundry room along with your huge hamper of stuff. I also think that for a hamper or large laundry bag find something you know you could carry to a room. Some people get ones on wheels and others just haul bags and look like Santa Claus. I had a traditional hamper, and sometimes when it was too full it was difficult to get downstairs, so make sure it's easy to carry up and down the stairs when it is full.

What else to buy or pack

This is the section where we will talk about technology, clothing, and immediate packing items that should be on your person!

When it comes to technology, you can pack as you please almost. You should definitely pack or buy a laptop. Some universities require certain laptops, and others don't care. Get what you feel comfortable with. If there are limitations for Mac users, please keep these in mind. I am personally a Mac user and have very few problems with my computer at school even though they prefer most people have PCs. Your computer will become your existence, since most of your schoolwork and communication will be online. If you want entertainment, such as TV and movies, I recommend you get a subscription to a video streaming service like Netflix. Along with your computer, make sure to pack your charger, a laptop case (unless your backpack will have enough room), and a rag to clean your screen with.

While on technology, the next thing you should pack is a printer. Most universities do not have wireless printing as an option; make sure to get one that relies on USB printing. I found it easiest to get the simplest, cheapest printer in existence so I would not have problems with complex settings or different sorts of options. My printer simply required paper and ink and had no menus or copy options: just printing. A printer is not necessarily required, but most places on campus charge for printing, and if someone on your floor wants to borrow your printer, you might just make a new friend!

Sometimes the Internet connection in your room or on campus is weak. Make sure to bring an Ethernet cable with you! The single room I had in spring semester had the worst Internet connection in the entire building so I was using that cable all the time, even though I never used it the previous semester.

If you are one of those people who downloads copyrighted materials illegally through torrents, I promise I won't get you in trouble and alert the authorities. What you do in your own time is your issue, but just so you don't get in trouble with the university, please disable these programs while on-campus. You could get in huge trouble for illegal downloads of any sort, so play it safe and *do not* use these technologies while on campus. Please be responsible!

The next important thing to pack is your cell phone and its charger. You will be keeping your cell phone with you all the time in case you get lost, meet new people, to check emails, etc.

Considering the amount of electronics you might be bringing to college, I would also recommend buying a power strip so you can increase the number of electrical outlets you have in one area. My power strip was near my desk and had my computer charger, phone charger, and lamp all in one!

When it comes to packing clothing, it is better to pack too much rather than too little since you can still send a lot home with your parents if you run out of room. Make sure to pack appropriately for the climate of where your university is. My university has very hot weather during the beginning of the fall semester, and by November it begins cooling off a bit so I had a couple of pairs of jeans and sweaters along with sundresses, shorts, and t-shirts. It might sound obvious, but if you are going to a big school or a school that has a lot of pride, pack or buy clothing that promotes your school's athletic teams. The essential college student realistically owns a lot of sweatpants, t-shirts, shorts, and casual clothing, as well as socks and undergarments. College is not usually a fashion show. Besides dressing for the weather, it is important to have some more formal clothing too. I'm not saying formal as in prom dress type formal (unless you are in a fraternity or sorority and are planning on going to a

Greek life formal), but formal as in interview attire. If you are a girl, bring a nice, conservative dress, or a skirt suit/pant suit, and if you're a guy, bring a suit and tie and a nice dress shirt and shoes. You will have more formal occasions that involve business attire than you're originally expecting, so I recommend having one outfit that you can depend on so you are prepared!

You should also have a backpack (and if you're a girl, a purse too) that you should be carrying when you move in. In your backpack should be the most important things you own: chargers, your laptop if it is not in its own case, and valuables. That way, anything important will not get lost. You will also have your wallet, keys, student ID, insurance card, and social security card on you at all times, and right now is when you are going to start doing this!

Try to avoid packing items that are very valuable or irreplaceable. Freshmen tend to make this mistake during the first couple of weeks. Many college students are aware of luxury items and theft in dorms does occur! It might not be your roommate, but it could be the girl down the hall or a friend of your roommate's that ends up looting your precious diamond studs you got for graduation. Unless you live alone and consistently lock your door (like I do, but even then I am wary because a housing staff member cleans the bathroom each Thursday when I am in class), stay away from bringing irreplaceable or extremely valuable items unless you will be wearing them at all times. I brought up a very nice purse when I lived alone, and I wear that purse every single day and take it everywhere with me so it is never at risk of getting stolen.

The last thing I advise you pack isn't really for you to keep up at college, but it is more for ease when move-in comes around. Tell your parents to bring a handcart or a dolly—something to help transport heavy things from your car, up an elevator, and into your room. This is especially helpful and saves time on items like a fridge and all the loaded storage boxes.

Important people

When you are getting ready to begin your new life in college, there are important people all over campus that you should get to know when you first begin, or right before you move.

The first important person you should meet (if necessary) is the person in charge of the disability office. This is the person that can help you receive accommodations in the dorms, introduce you to housing staff, get you a note-taker in class, more test time, or help pair you with an older student mentor. Having contact with this person will save you a lot of time in the future. If you don't feel as if you need accommodations, knowing this person will still provide you with a friendly face on campus; they will know you, and if you do need something later on, they can help you.

The next important person you should meet if you live on campus is your RA. I didn't meet or know who my RA was until the first day I moved in. Your RA is is a university employed older student who is there to help you find opportunities on campus, resolve problems, answer questions, or even be a friend. Sometimes they organize social activities so all of the residents get to know each other better. On the first day when you are moving in, your family might get to meet your RA as well. If you feel it is necessary, advocate for yourself and let your RA know about your challenges. They are supposed to be there to listen and help you succeed during the year, so if they are aware, they will always be attentive if a problem arises and might make sure to keep things social or have more ice breakers in the beginning so you can get to meet your neighbors.

Accommodations

If you are on a difference-friendly campus, you might be able to get accommodations. Once you meet all the important people on campus who will be able to help you, it is time to start getting accommodations if you need them. One of the most important accommodations, if you ask me, is with housing. I mentioned my fear of having a roommate and my autism getting in the way, so I spoke to someone in housing. When things with my roommate did not work as planned, my contact in housing was also the person who was able to get me a single room in the same building on campus. Being able to get to live with someone who is a good match for you, or being able to get a private/ single bedroom, is probably one of the best things a student with autism can do in my opinion, because you are still able to keep your privacy, follow your own schedule without depending on somebody else's, and live the way you want to. It eliminates the entire roommate factor completely.

Other than housing, the largest portion of accommodations you can receive from a college or university are in academics. Getting accommodations almost always guarantees you will have to talk to your professor about them during the first week of school, so on the positive side, you will definitely get to know your professor and have the opportunity to talk to them no matter how many students are in your class. In order to receive academic accommodations, you will take advantage of the people you spoke to at the disability office. They will probably have records of your diagnosis or academic issues from your high school or your parents. Academic accommodations usually include things such as extra time on tests, being able to meet with your professors more often outside of class, having a test in a different format, or anything that is reasonable and doable to help you succeed in your coursework. One of the best accommodations I know people get that could be helpful for students on the spectrum is getting to take your tests somewhere quiet in a different location during regular test time. Basically, you get to take them with no distractions instead of in the same room as hundreds of people and have less sensory input, and just the peace and quiet of your own space and being able to think.

I do not personally get any academic accommodations but I do have my diagnosis and information on file with the disability office in case I ever do need anything in the future.

"Summer of learning"

I like to call the summer before college the "summer of learning," because this is the summer where you are going to practice being an adult while you are still home. This is the time when you are going to learn a lot of the things your parents do for you and you probably take for granted, such as cooking, laundry, driving places, etc. Of course, since you are still home, your parents will be able to help you and give you feedback as you are learning. It's the first step to independent living, so get excited and prepare to learn a lot!

You may or may not need to learn to cook in college. If you have an apartment or access to a full kitchen, you might feel more inclined to make your own meals. If you have a community kitchen with an oven like my dorm does, cooking might not be for you. It wasn't for me, and I don't really know how to yet. However, my mom (who should be a gourmet chef) always told me, "If you can read, you can cook," so I'm hoping that someday I can pick up a book full of recipes and make something edible without burning or ruining it. If you plan on cooking in college and sharing ovens and equipment, I would recommend learning simple, quick recipes. There were people on my floor who would make dishes that took hours and many other residents were upset since they wanted to use the kitchen as well. Some of the easy recipes that I've seen people make and that have no complaints are baked chicken and chocolate chip cookies since they take no longer than about 20 minutes. I figure anything that comes as premade dough, roll, or mix should be pretty simple to make and not take too much time out of your day or make others annoyed with you.

During my "summer of learning," laundry was one of the most important things I learned how to do. With laundry, you're going to learn to use all the detergents, sorting, cycle settings, timing, and folding. Your dorm building will have its own laundry room, and the washing machines and dryers might be different than what you have at home. Check your college's website if they have specifics so you know what will be different and if you will be using anything different. Ask your parents to walk you through a few loads, or, if you learn better from following directions, ask them to write out a list of instructions to follow so you can wash and dry your clothes. Definitely ask for help on folding though—I still think it's hard, so I think having your parents show you how they do it is very helpful since folding is a very visual concept.

If you are bringing a car to college or commuting, you might want to brush up on your driving skills. If you are out of town the roads might be harder to drive on, or more difficult. Make sure you know your directions and if needed, have a navigation system in case you get lost. If you are planning on driving and don't feel prepared yet, go out with your parents and practice driving and parking. With experience comes confidence, so keep driving until you feel more comfortable!

If there is anything else that you feel uncomfortable with before you leave and want to master, such as setting an alarm clock and waking up early, now is your time to try it and get it down to a science so you won't struggle while at school!

Orientation and registration

Before you begin school, you will have to attend an orientation and registration session. At orientation, you are usually getting to know the university and getting excited about being a student. You might get to go on another campus tour and meet current and new students. Orientation at my college was a two-day, very social event where we had to stay in the dorms overnight. I was stuck in a triple room with two girls who were already best friends. It was very uncomfortable for me, and I got my parents to pick me up and take me back to their hotel room. During the day, we were divided into small groups to learn about the university and what it had to offer. We learned about all the different departments that offered specific majors, and about issues that commonly affected college students as well as resources to help us. We also had a parent orientation so parents could learn about what their children are going through, and financial planning seminars.

At registration, you will get to meet with an advisor to help you pick your classes for your first semester based on university requirements, interests, and path of study. Your classes during the first semester are much more broad and generalized than the classes you will take later in your college career. You won't be taking major-specific classes straight away (most likely), since you need to take basic courses in order to eventually take advanced courses. Advisors will also typically tell you to take a lighter course load during your first semester so you can transition and get used to college-level work and the lifestyle of a college student. During your first semester, you will be the most social you will ever be during your college career because everyone is looking for friends in the beginning. There are also lots of different involvement opportunities and club meetings that happen in the beginning of the fall. If you go to a large university, it is also the season for major sporting events like football and some basketball, so you might be interested in going to games on the weekends. If an average workload for a semester is 15 credit hours (about five classes), most freshman take between 12–16 credits (four or five classes and a lab, possibly) during the first semester so they can get used to college and enjoy all their new home has to offer. Once registration is over, you are well on your way to moving in and beginning your journey to your ideal career!

When picking courses, you could also consider arranging your schedule based on what times of day would suit you best. If getting up early in the morning in high school drained you or you were the kid who used to fall asleep in class, try to get classes later in the morning or during the afternoon, or even night classes. If you're a morning person, morning classes will be good for you. Honestly, the best perk for me about early morning classes is that they tend to be smaller because more students who sign up for them tend to skip by oversleeping or a lack of motivation to get dressed and out of bed, or that morning classes are unpopular. Consider your sleep habits when choosing classes so they fit you and you are wide awake, able to focus, and have the time you need to get things done.

Every time I make a schedule (I've done it four times already: freshman fall, spring and summer, and sophomore fall), I consider when I'm awake, how interesting the course sounds (which could determine whether I want to wake up for a morning class), and who is teaching the class. A professor could make or break the class, so if the registrar has the professor or teacher's name available online, you could search for previous semester's syllabi, ask older students, or check a source as such www.ratemyprofessor.com to find out how hard the class is and if they are a good instructor. A bad instructor may not suit your learning style or make a class unnecessarily difficult, so beware, and sometimes you might be sacrificing a good schedule to get a better instructor and a better chance of an "A" in the class.

CHAPTER 3

DORM LIFE 101

Lots of people have told me that dorm life for at least one year is essential to an ideal college experience. You get to experience living close to someone whose world you may have never known otherwise, be ridiculously close to your classes/workplace, and in lots of cases, share bathrooms with ridiculous amounts of people. How often do you get to become so close to a complete stranger (assuming your roommate is random or not someone you've known your whole life)?

Dorm life, however, also has a very artificial feeling. You call maintenance people and they show up, if you have problems you talk to a resident assistant, you lack a lot of things a real apartment has such as your own laundry machine inside of your room, or your own kitchen, and there's no true responsibility or ownership. However, dorm life in my opinion is halfway between living in a bedroom in your parents' house and having your own place. It's very nice, very social, and very comfortable.

But dorm life also has a lot of variables and whatnot, and that's why this section is here—because dorm life isn't as simple as here's a room, a roommate, and go live here like it's a hotel room.

Residence hall setups

If you live on campus, you live in a dorm or residence hall. If you are one of those people who are starting school during the summer, you will probably live somewhere different in the fall than you do in the summer. Some residence halls are reserved for upperclassmen, and those are usually filled with single rooms or four-person apartments: setups that are much more desirable for older students who are focused on their upper-level coursework and preparing for careers. As an incoming freshman, you will probably be living in a double (with one roommate) or a triple (with two roommates).

I want to stress, as I stressed in the packing sections, that space is limited, in triples especially. Triple rooms are typically not much bigger than doubles and have another person in them, and in order to make more space, two of the roommates might bunk their beds.

Move-in

After lots of packing and preparation, it is finally time to move into your room! If you have a roommate, coordinate with them who will move in first. If you both move in at the same time, the room you share might become very crowded with two people's stuff coming in at once, as well as two families sharing a small space at the same time. I recommend that if you both want to move in on the same day, one of you moves in during the morning and the other moves in at night. That way, one family could occupy the room at a time. It is also nice because if you are the morning shift, you could hang out with your family and go out to dinner together at night, since this is one of those moments you will share together in your college town before they go back home and you begin living away from home. If you are on the night shift, it is also easier to move in because the hot summer sun won't be out and it is less crowded. There are also more resources available to you, such as less crowded elevators, carts, dollies, and other move-in supplies.

If your college is a reasonable driving distance from home (less than one day), I recommend you evaluate your driving situation. If you are bringing your own car to college, see how much your car could hold. If your car doesn't hold a lot, you could take two cars (your parents' and yours). However, my best advice is to rent a van from a rental car service since you are able to fit a ton of stuff inside of it. During move-in, we loaded up our SUV to the brim: the entire trunk and back seat was full, it was very cramped, and we even had one of those skyboxes on top of the roof. It still barely fit all my stuff in it! When I moved out in the spring, we rented a van and were able to fit everything inside of it with no issue, and we did not have to worry about our car getting stuffed or having problems because of all the things inside of it. For my next move-in, we are also renting a van to keep everything simple and doable!

When you are moving in, it is important to be organized. When you pack, you should be aware of what you are packing, and if you use storage boxes, you should label them or be able to identify what is inside of each of them. Try to do one section of your side of the room at a time: for instance, start with the desk area and then move onto the bedding and storage underneath the bed. Decorating should always be last so all the important stuff is inside of the room and organized first! If you have to share space with your roommate and you are the first to move in, I recommend dividing some of that space in half. I had to share some drawers near our mirror with my roommate, so I took two and she got two. I was first, so I chose the two drawers I would rather have as "mine." Try to be respectful and fair since you will probably be living together for the rest of the year. If your roommate agrees with you that he or she doesn't need the same amount of space you do, then feel free to take over some extra drawers or storage space once it is okay with both of you.

Once your space is completely unpacked, organized, and decorated, congratulations! Feel free to admire your new home. I recommend taking pictures on the day you move in so your parents can show off to your family and friends back home, and because your room will never look any better than it does on move-in day. I know this for a fact because the more you live in your room, the messier it becomes. Try to keep the room clean and organized in the beginning so everyone's efforts and hard work that first day don't go to waste, but between you and me, we know it won't look like that first day for the first semester, let alone the entire year.

Buying and selling textbooks

When you first arrive on campus, your parents are probably going to be like mine and encourage you to be proactive in buying textbooks before classes even begin. As a new student, you're probably going to end up like me and buy all your books brand new for full price at the on-campus bookstore. A year later, I can tell you that is not the way to go! My first textbook bill came close to $600, and I was shocked that books were so expensive. What I then learned are some of the best money-saving and efficient ways to buy (and sell) textbooks, so you will be a seasoned pro in no time!

First, I recommend you check the syllabi for all your classes before buying the textbooks. If the syllabus isn't specific enough about the requirements, you should wait until the first day of class. Some classes say the book is absolutely required, and others say it is optional. If it is optional, consider whether having the book will be beneficial. If it is a math class, I say buy the book if it's optional so you can access all the practice problems and get clarification on the lessons if you need it. Sometimes, the syllabus for a class might even note if an older edition will suffice for the book. If so, buy the older edition! The older editions are much cheaper and almost all of the information is the same, except for some page numbers and small updates on current events and research. I wouldn't recommend going back more than three editions though. The more editions backwards you move from the current one, the more outdated the information will be. Don't buy a first edition if the required book is an eleventh edition, for instance—but the ninth or tenth edition is most likely acceptable in this case.

If you can, buy the textbooks used. Used textbooks can be an asset because the person who owned the book before you may have highlighted the book and pointed out what was important to them while they were studying for the class! However, this could be bad if the person was "highlighter happy" and highlighted the entire book, or if you are easily distracted by highlighting. If you are buying a used book from the bookstore, the condition of the book is usually pretty good and the highlighting should be responsible. Of course, used books are cheaper.

If you aren't buying from a bookstore, there are other options for used books. You could order them online if you are given the title, author, and/or ISBN number. Usually the prices online are pretty good as well. For textbooks, a lot of people buy from websites such as Chegg and Amazon and get them delivered to their homes before they leave for move-in, or get them delivered to their dorms.

The best way to buy textbooks, in my opinion, is usually to buy from other students who have previously taken the course. These students have probably highlighted the book, pointed out what is important, and are impatient to sell the book so they can buy their books for next semester. Buying books from students is almost always a bargain, because in my experience they charge a maximum of half of what the bookstore charges for the book. Be aware that students almost always accept only cash for books, so if you are planning on putting your book expenses on a credit or debit card, this might not be the route for you. While you are meeting with the student you are buying from, you could also ask plenty of questions about the class and have an advantage of knowing what the professor is like and how to study. If you are looking for students to buy from, your best bet is actually Facebook. If your graduation class or your proposed major have a page, many students advertise what books they are selling and for how much money. Conversely, you could advertise which books you are buying and hope people message you with prices if they have those books for sale. If you want to buy from students, just send a Facebook message and plan on when to meet up. As usual, be careful with online safety during these transactions, and see if you can validate they are students before agreeing to buy.

There is also the option to rent textbooks. I personally think renting textbooks is not a good idea, since when you buy a textbook, keep in mind you will probably sell it after you are done with the course, so you will be getting some of your purchase price back (if not all of it) when you resell the book. When you rent, you are just throwing money away and have to give the book back to the renter at the end, and if you drop the course, your situation just becomes an unfortunate throwing away of money.

The only time you should be buying books brand new is if they come in a bundled package. By a package, I mean the book is included as well as a course-required CD-ROM and/or access codes to online software. This is the only case where it is in your favor to buy the book new, because if you buy the book used and the access codes and CDs separately, it will end up costing you more money and time because you need to order those things either online or directly from the publisher for full price.

Sometimes, courses also offer the option of e-books or online textbooks. If you could learn with this medium, by all means pursue it, but I'm not sure if you would be able to resell, highlight, or get all the benefits of a hard-copy textbook. This situation depends mostly upon how you learn, so do what benefits your learning style and study habits most!

When selling your books at the end of the semester, you will be following a lot of the same procedures that buying has, only in reverse. You can sell your books back to the bookstore if they are in decent condition, and you might not get offered as much money as a student might pay you. You can also list your books for sale on Amazon or another selling site. And of course, if you advertise on social media such as Facebook, you can coordinate selling it to another student. Sometimes, though, being on the selling end takes more time since you are waiting for a buyer to come along. Also, the one thing I learned is the earlier you sell your books, the more money you might make before the supply goes up and the demand goes down. There is one book I sold my first semester that I got $20 more for than the average price because I was one of the first students to sell the book to students taking the course in the spring. I try to sell my books before or during finals week: if the book wasn't necessary for studying, I'll sell it before finals week for top dollar, and if I need it to study, I'll advertise it for sale the week before but meet up to sell it the day of my final or the day after the final. I've sold enough books and met up with enough people over the past year that it eventually becomes routine at the end of the semester, and if you buy/sell through students, your textbooks could cost you close to nothing if you use similar pricing and don't heavily damage the books.

Meeting your neighbors

When you live in a dorm, typically your floor is going to be single-gender (mine was the only building on campus that didn't follow this trend). You will be living in close quarters with around 30 other boys or girls, so it is essential to get to know as many of them as possible. Many dorms are social, so during the first few weeks, I recommend hanging out and doing work in the common space or lounge your floor has so you can see all the different residents as they pass by and possibly strike up some friendly conversations. You don't have to like or be friends with everyone, but always be friendly! Say hello to everyone you know, and ask how they are doing.

Your RA will most likely host a mandatory floor meeting during the first week of classes. During this meeting, he or she will go over essential dorm rules, such as fire safety, and explain how he or she is there for you to talk to, answer questions, and to help you. Your RA will also want the floor to be a community together, so he or she will also make everyone introduce themselves or play some icebreaker games so everyone gets to know each other a little bit better. You will also have floor meetings throughout the year, so at that time you are more than welcome to continue getting to know everyone since the meetings are mandatory. The mandatory meetings tend to bring out the people you don't see around the dorms very often in my experience; you might see people you've never seen before (this actually happened to me at the last meeting of the year).

Meeting your neighbors is especially important since a lot of people really do meet amazing friends on their freshman dorm floor. I know I did. I met my best friend because he lived on my floor. I wouldn't have met him if I had not been outside in the common area chatting with another person during the first week.

Roommate issues

I hate to be the bearer of bad news, but more than likely you and your roommate are not going to have a perfect relationship no matter how much you enjoyed talking to each other over the summer or how similar your living habits are. Roommate issues are very real, and nearly everyone encounters some sort of conflict with their roommates. That's why, in the beginning of the fall semester, my RA had each set of roommates come up with some ground rules and agreements to return to her with signatures from both roommates.

One of the most common roommate problems overall is a difference in schedules. You might have an early morning class, but your roommate doesn't have class until noon. Your roommate might be a lighter sleeper who gets upset when your alarm goes off so you don't skip class. You might also go to bed three hours earlier (or later) than your roommate. However, if you ask me, the best advice is to be respectful to each other. If you stay up later and your roommate is sleeping, try not to leave all the lights on, or go to a common area or somewhere else (but somewhere safe, of course!) to study so you don't wake them.

Another set of problems that I've seen happen is caused by social habits. Your roommate may want his or her significant other to spend the night, or have sex in the room. If this is not okay with you, put your foot down before it happens, or if you don't care what your roommate does when you aren't home, make sure there is some sort of code that means you're not allowed in because of these sorts of things (this is much more common with guys than girls, from my experience). You or your roommate might also enjoy going out at night to clubs or parties, and get back insanely late. There are also the issues of underage drinking that occur. Some people party harder (and more illegally, if you are under 21) than others. If an incident happens and a conflict arises and you two can't come to a resolution, talk to your RA about what is going on. If you are worried about your roommate drinking too much or partying too hard, talk to your RA, and if needed, the two of you can get additional help for your roommate through support groups and resources to help prevent an alcohol or drug problem.

You and your roommate may also have conflict regarding your autism. Maybe the smells of their perfumes or colognes are overpowering your sense of space, they like having people over often, or they might blast their music at unspeakable levels. A lot of these might not be problems for others, but they might be for you. It is important to be aware of which things will set you off (loud noises, bright lights, smells) and if you trust your roommate, have an open and honest discussion if you choose to disclose your diagnosis to him or her. Your roommate will be more likely to accommodate your differences if they know why some of their habits might bother you so much. Of course, when you confront something sensory or something else that you know causes you to act a certain way because of your autism, be kind and respectful, and if you think it will make things easier, offer some suggestions (such as, "Could you possibly spray your perfume in the bathroom instead of in our room?" or, "Could you maybe use headphones or keep the volume down a little bit when I'm home as well?" or, "Would you let me know when you're going to have a bunch of people over so I can give you guys your space?"). Being supportive and understanding of yourself will help your roommate feel the same way. If you need more help, do not hesitate to reach out to your RA to help you both set some ground rules and agreements regarding this topic.

Keep in mind as well that your roommate is not the person designed to be your new best friend. As long as you two are able to get along without issues, solve conflicts together when they arise, and are respectful, you should have a good year together.

To disclose or not to disclose?

Let's just say I'm not the first college student out there who has autism, so the issue of whether or not to disclose to people you meet is very real. I chose to disclose to the university and others, and I know people with an ASD who never said a word while in college. I often wonder if I made the right decisions of who to disclose to and educate, even considering this is my second book and my story is available for anyone to read. Anyone who wanted to know about my autism could easily find out without me saying a word. However, disclosure is an intimate thing. For me, disclosing was a sign of trust and reaching out throughout the years, and it still is when it comes to social situations and people since most just regard it as part of me and move on like it is taboo to talk about.

If you do choose to disclose for academic reasons, then definitely talk to the people in charge of disability resources on campus so you can get the accommodations you need, or if you ever need anything to benefit your experience, they will be able to help you because they have your information and diagnosis on file. If you disclose academically, there is no need to tell your peers anything unless you want to.

Personally, the next person I would disclose to other than disability resources or the Dean's office would be the RA. Your RA is there to help you no matter what, and in most cases they are trained to help all students through their difficulties and conflicts. If something ever comes up with your roommate, or you need some help or feel lost, your RA might be friendlier to you or more likely to give you a hand if they understand the types of challenges you are going through. I wished I met with my RA earlier during the fall to explain how difficult college was with autism and the types of challenges I had before I went in to talk to her about roommate conflict. At this point, she said something to me along the lines of, "I had no idea how hard it was for you here or how your situation was with your autism," and it was then I wished I had asked for help or at least given a better heads-up education beforehand. She knew I had autism, but didn't understand the majority of the picture involved. A lot of people today are like that if they don't know someone personally with autism, especially a high-functioning version of it—they know the word and are familiar with the severe end of the spectrum, but do not quite get how students with HFA or AS are affected. It is up to you to advocate and educate the people around you if you want to either make changes or get the help and understanding you need.

However, when it comes to roommates, that's where I really begin to question if disclosing is a good idea. I feel like you really need to figure out what kind of person your roommate is before you disclose. If your roommate realizes your autism and your personality are those of a naïve people-pleaser (like me), there is a good chance they will take advantage of you. Most people with autism want to be liked, have a friend, and avoid conflict at any cost. Unfortunately, if you are too much of a people-pleaser, you could get manipulated and taken advantage of, ultimately getting you in trouble and looking like the bad one of the two of you. You might be lending things and doing favors you wouldn't normally do or agree out of fear of conflict, or just to be liked. Basically, unless you are completely sure it would benefit you (your roommate might help you get organized, introduce you to friends, or even be a better listener), I would really think long and hard about disclosing in this case.

When it comes to friends, I honestly have no problem disclosing. I look at it as a great way of weeding out people who won't like me for me, or who don't want to be there in case I do have sensory overload, or any other sorts of problems. Some people run away when they hear "autism" because they hear media stereotypes, or think you might be violent after allegations on the news of certain murderers possibly having AS.

One story of friendship and my autism was when I actually had a sensory overload problem in college when I went to a basketball game. I went with my friend, and my ears would not stop ringing and I wanted nothing more than to leave. The arena was overwhelming for me and the acoustics were terrible. We all have friends who would probably encourage us to "tough it out" and stay to watch the rest of the game, but my friend was really cool and said he didn't think the game was that great, and we left and laughed about how we didn't really like basketball anyway. He was more than understanding about the situation at hand and on that night I realized which parts of my autism could affect friendships. If you don't disclose, that's okay too. Just remember, if your friend is a true friend, it won't affect your friendship negatively—think of the expression, "Those who matter don't mind, and those who mind don't matter." It is ultimately your decision whether or not you want your friends to know.

Avoiding isolation

Let me just say this is a weird, but important, section for me to write. I live in a single room and becoming isolated is a very real issue for me since I don't have to rush off to a common area or library to go study because I can just shut my door. I also don't have community bathrooms so I don't have to see a group of girls every time I shower or brush my teeth. I also live in an honors dorm that isn't very social to begin with, so I could sometimes go days without seeing anyone. However, isolation is not an integral part of the college experience, and I want to help you avoid falling into the same pitfalls I fell into during my freshman spring.

To avoid isolation, you don't exactly need to have friends. I usually explain my social life at college by saying that I probably know at least 100 people from different organizations, retreats, and areas of campus, but I truly consider myself friends with one or two people. Despite my lack of friends and large amount of acquaintances, I don't participate in lots of social functions.

I know everyone I know through two retreats I went on during the spring semester, a network of the top 25 freshman leaders at my university, where I live, and the clubs and organizations I am a part of.

If you are studying and want to be social, I recommend joining study groups for your classes or going to the library at a medium-quiet spot. Study groups help you talk about and teach what you are learning to others and it could help you, and if the group gets off-topic or social before or after, you would most likely be invited to dinner afterwards or to go get a snack, etc. The library has a tendency to be a social scene in college. Lots of people want to be seen studying. Each floor in a college library has a designated quiet level—most typically for each college I toured, the higher floors are quieter than the lower floors. If you go to the library to study, I recommend you put yourself together, look nice, and pick a spot that is quiet enough for you to study, but could be loud enough for someone to talk to you or whisper without causing a commotion.

If you're bored on campus and don't want to stay in your room and isolate yourself, see what kind of fun events are going on around campus. Friday nights are usually the busiest time. I find it's best to see what's going on at the student union since that is usually the hub of campus life. The student union might have free movies, free food, or other events going on for you to participate in. If you don't want to go alone, bring up an event or activity with a friend, or even tell your RA about it: there's a chance your RA will make it an event for everyone and your floor could go, for instance.

Meal plans/food

Most freshmen have meal plans, either by choice or requirement. Meal plans allow students to eat at the on-campus dining halls, and depending on your meal plan, you might get three meals a day. A meal plan is great because it eases all your concerns about eating and buying food—you just show up and get lots of food that was prepaid when you signed up for a meal plan.

The best thing about meal plans isn't the "all you can eat" buffet style that dining halls tend to embrace, but the fact that many other freshmen have a meal plan. Because most freshmen have meal plans, either out of requirement or by choice, the dining halls are often very social. When I first moved in, everyone in my dorm would try to go to dinner at the same time because everyone had a meal plan, so there was always someone to sit with. At the beginning of the semester, nobody really knows each other, so it is perfectly okay to sit with someone you don't know or to join a new group. You will be surprised by how many people you can meet in the dining hall, and as the year progresses, how many familiar faces you will end up seeing!

If you do not have a meal plan and have no interest in going to the dining hall, it is important to weigh up your other options. If you have on-campus restaurants outside of a dining hall or restaurants fairly close to campus, you could eat there. If you have a car, it's time to be an adult and learn to shop for groceries to keep in your room or to help prepare to cook a meal. If you don't have a car and want to go grocery shopping, see if any grocery store is within walking distance, and if not, ask a friend who has a car to take you shopping with them.

I did not have a meal plan since I didn't think the food was very good during my orientation, which is when meal plan signups were. Instead, I had an account with the university that was tied to my debit card and allowed me a certain amount of money to spend on food. With that card, I was still able to get into the dining hall, but I had to pay each time I went. At the beginning of the semester, I would go to the dining hall three nights a week, or if someone I knew wanted to go. I had my fair share of dining hall pizza (they had pizza every night!) and sat with groups of strangers, joined friends, and sometimes just went between classes because it was quick and on the way back to the dorm or to my next class.

For my sophomore year, I have access to a car so I am planning on going grocery shopping more often. I was able to go to the grocery store during my freshman year by taking a city bus that left campus, but I was limited in how much I could carry and bring back. When I made those infrequent trips to the store, I would empty out my backpack so I could bring more items and food home with me when I went to the store, since I figured with only two hands to help me carry things, I could only carry about four bags of groceries which wasn't usually enough to last a while. The backpack used to be ideal for carrying heavier things like a jug of milk, while my hands held the lighter packages.

Exploring campus

Now that you are all moved in before the first day of class, this is your ideal time to go explore campus and figure out where everything is. This usually makes for a great social event if you want to get to know more freshmen who might be lost like yourself. What most freshmen do, a day or two before classes, is to travel in groups looking for all the different buildings on their schedules so they know how to get there. If you want to do this alone, that's okay too, and it might be more accurate so you can account for the time it realistically takes to get from one class to the next if they are back to back.

While you're exploring campus, I highly recommend you go inside of a lot of the buildings you have class in, including auditoriums if they are empty. Buildings might have odd numbering for room numbers, or have a floor below ground to further confuse students. When you see the room where class is held (even if you are not allowed inside yet), you might get a better idea of how many students are in your class. If you do have large lecture classes at your university, they are held in auditoriums. Auditorium courses could have hundreds of students, and when you are in there alone you will definitely be able to imagine the sheer number of students that will show up to class on the first day.

During your investigation of campus, look for good study spots. A good study spot is accessible and safe at nighttime. By safe, I mean it is on a well-lit path, people are nearby or there is a short, direct route to get back to your dorm. A good study spot could be very important if you have difficulty studying in the dorms or need quiet space. While you're on this hunt, definitely look inside of the libraries and get a feel of where is a quiet place that you could use to focus on your work—chances are, that's where you will find a study spot you could use throughout the year.

CHAPTER 4

ACADEMICS

I know a lot of people who originally fall into two (and a half) camps when they arrive at college or begin to fill out an application. The first group of young people have already planned and are convinced of their lives' directions: they already have a solid idea of what their major will be, what kind of career they want, and where they will pursue their undergraduate and graduate studies. The second camp is people who have no idea what they want to do except they either want to go to college, or their parents are simply expecting them to go to college. There is also the middle ground of kids who have faint ideas of want they want to do, but haven't decided on one thing, and see themselves doing multiple things, but have no real idea of what they actually want to do four years from now.

I fell into the middle ground group. I found it very scary to be certain of what I wanted to do by October of my senior year. I wanted to keep writing, keep drawing, and find some kind of professional career that would let me do that since I didn't believe that writing and drawing would be a feasible career as a real adult.

Considering that my art is incorporated under HaleyMossART, Inc., I demonstrated an interest in pursuing a business degree and maybe even getting a Master's of Business Administration (MBA) on my college applications. One of the schools I applied to offered a three-year undergraduate program, and I would get the MBA in my fourth year. It all sounded like a good plan. By the time my acceptance letters began coming in, as early as Halloween and as late as mid-March, I didn't exactly want to be a business major. I finally believed I had the confidence and brains to become a doctor—I wanted to be a psychiatrist, specifically, so I could help diagnose kids with autism and console their families as they grieved, and then tell them here I was before them, a woman with autism, and a beacon of hope.

Then, when I got to freshman orientation, I considered a degree in graphic design because of my longstanding interest in art and love of working with digital media. That lasted about two days when I realized the art buildings were located off-campus and I might not be happy with art as a full-time career. At orientation I was required to declare a major to sign up for courses, so I chose psychology since I still wanted to be an inspiring psychiatrist.

Two months later, I decided on a goal I could achieve after dropping my first chemistry class on the doctor path: psychology major, but pre-law. Now I want to go to law school and be in disability law to help protect and advocate for those with disabilities, and I'm pretty sure that's where I want to end up.

I know people who have changed majors nearly five or six times in one year. The important thing here is if your academics aren't up to snuff or you're not taking the right courses, you might not get the opportunities you want. Your grades must be good to get into specific majors and programs, and good grades will grant you the freedom needed to change your mind or move forward. Academics open doors, and hopefully, with a little bit of advice, guidance, and luck, you'll find and end up exactly where you want to be.

Majors, minors, etc.

Once again, let's face it: academics are the real reason you're in college, not to live away, gain experience on your own, or party like a rock star. The biggest commitment you have while in college are your academics, and preparing for the rest of your life in a career you ideally will love. The first step to training for the career of your dreams is choosing a major that will help you get into those kinds of jobs and careers and will allow you to pursue your interests. A major is a concentrated area of study that will ultimately end up on your degree, and it is where the majority of your specialized classes will be taken. Colleges offer many different majors for a variety of careers, ranging from different types of engineering to graphic design. The larger your university is, the more majors are offered.

Typically, you will have to declare a major during your second or third year of college. However, many students change majors as they take more classes and learn about different subjects they may have never found interesting until learning more. It is important to keep an open mind while selecting courses and learning about new things.

If you have a wide range of interests and want an academic challenge, you could declare two majors. If you declare two majors, make sure to meet with an advisor or two to make sure it is feasible and you will graduate on time. However, if you do choose two specializations, be aware that you won't get as much time or room in your schedule to explore new interests or courses you wanted to take. Plan accordingly if this is something that interests you!

As I said, I began college at a psychology major, but before I decided that, I really was unsure about what I wanted to study because I have a wide range of interests. I chose psychology not exactly because I want to be a psychologist, but because there are many different options out there: if I want, I could get a masters degree or a PhD and go into counseling, research, forensic psychology, be a professor, or go on to law school (which is currently my plan).

The next cool thing you could do when planning your academic career is you could add a minor (or multiple minors). Minors are smaller specializations—usually about five classes, give or take, and are usually more fun if you ask me. Minors can be very specific and more interest-concentrated.

Career goals (jobs, graduate school, etc.)

After giving some thought to your major, you might also want to give your future goals some thought as well. Depending on what you want to do with your life, this determines what kind of major you might choose and what courses you will take.

If you are going for a specific career or job, meet with someone who is in that career or a career planning service to see how you feel about it and what you are required to take. It is always a good idea to see exactly what you are getting into, and you could possibly get a job or internship out of your resources! If you are unsure of the requirements for your college, meet with an advisor so they can help you out.

If you are pursuing a pre-health professional program, regardless of your major, keep in mind that you are required to take certain courses or their equivalents for your application into a professional program (medical school, pharmacy school, dental school, nursing school, etc.). These types of programs usually require chemistry, biology, organic chemistry, physics, and other sciences, so make sure you know exactly what you need and how well you need to do. You will also need to score well on graduate entrance exams, depending on the program, so make sure you think about time to study for those.

If you are pursuing a pre-law professional program, there is no ideal coursework or major for getting into law school. It is up to you to succeed in your classes, and score well on a law school admissions exam (the LSAT, typically). Like those of you pursuing a science, make sure to study hard for your entrance exams! A liberal arts education is most typical for those who are applying to law school as it teaches you the required set of thinking and writing skills to succeed in the legal field.

In other programs, graduate school might be something you want to pursue. Doctoral (PhD) and masters degrees might be something that you might look into in order to get a better paying job, because you want to stay in school longer, or it is necessary to get where you want to be. If this is something you are interested in, look at the types of entrance exam requirements needed, and make sure you are following your undergraduate course of study as well.

Just remember, no matter what you want to do, keep up your grades so you have the option to go to graduate school if that is something you want! Good grades also get you internships and job offers. Keep in mind that your grades will open or close doors for you so try your best and work hard so you can do what you would like to do!

Class sizes and aiming for the best seat

Depending on the size of your university, and the difficulty level of courses you are taking, the classes will also vary in size. This section will help you to cope with large classes and get the most out of a small class.

Most freshmen classes are typically very general in subject matter (such as calculus, chemistry, introductory psychology) because a lot of different majors and career paths require these courses, or the university has a universal foundation requirement that all students eventually participate in them. These kinds of classes are usually held in auditoriums, and can hold hundreds of students: each auditorium course I took held between 200 and 500 students. It is dependent on the instructor whether or not they take attendance (in the case of hundreds of students, it is done electronically). If they do not take attendance, it is your responsibility either to go to class or learn the material yourself. If you do not go to class for whatever reason, you'll still need to know what was covered in lectures, so either have friends in class or rely on the textbook or other outside sources to succeed. I am not giving you an excuse to skip class, but sometimes you might not feel as if you have a choice (you need to study for another class, you overslept, something happened). If not showing up is something you have to do, just remember you are an adult and what you do reflects on you, not your parents or anyone else.

Of course though, I hope you are a conscientious, good student and do go to class. It will make your life easier and you are paying for it through tuition anyways. But if you are overwhelmed by the number of students, it is time to decide where to sit. It can be hard to judge where the best place to sit in a large lecture hall is. Sometimes it might seem like a good idea to sit up front so you don't have to worry about seeing hundreds of people, but when class is over, you will have to fight your way through a crowd of hundreds to leave. If the auditorium is on a slant of sorts like a movie theatre, I find it best to sit towards the middle so you don't have to crane your neck up too much, there is still a large group of people behind you, and it is not a long ordeal to leave class. If you are sick that day but still need to or want to go to class, I would sit towards the back in case you have to leave. That way, you won't disrupt the class if you feel too sick to stay.

However, as you progress through your college career and begin taking major-specific courses, your classes will begin to dwindle in size. Your classes will go from hundreds to a maximum of about 50. You will get to ask questions with more ease, your professor will know your name, and you will most likely know the classmates you have. If you go to a small college, or are in a special program, you might have small classes during your entire college career.

Professors, teaching assistants, and graduate students

While you are in college, there are different types of people who could be teaching your courses, ranging from a student who is several years older than you, to a graduate student, or a tenured professor. The size and subject of the class will determine who teaches your class, and their approachability.

A tenured professor is the typical college professor. They are usually a respected adult who does research for the university as well as publishing articles, journals, and books about the subjects they teach. Professors may even write the textbook for the class they teach because they are truly experts in the field. They tend to teach very large or specialized classes, but do not teach everything. A professor may also have assigned teaching assistants (TAs) to answer questions so their emails don't get spammed, or to direct traffic since large classes could mean large amounts of work on the professor's end. Chances are, unless the class is very small, you won't know your professor and they won't know you.

Undergraduate TAs are not as common because they are unpaid, volunteer students who get to teach a class or help a professor or graduate student teaching assistant. Typically, undergraduate TAs are upperclassmen who took the course they are helping with and did very well (usually a high A). An undergraduate TA usually does not have the same amount of power that a graduate student or a professor has, but they (in my opinion) seem more approachable because they are usually only a year or two older than you. These are the people to ask questions if they grade your papers or if you have a question about the course.

Graduate TAs are students who are usually pursuing their PhD or master's degrees and teach classes for credit. They often act like professors because they teach the classes, but they are not experts in the field. Larger universities utilize more graduate teaching assistants because it is a labor pool already there, and that way, the professors can teach the more important, larger classes, and use their time to do research and publish findings. Graduate students can be a lot like regular teachers; either they are very nice or very strict. Some are far more approachable than others since they are very close in age to you (every graduate student who taught me last year was probably no older than 25). The classes that graduate students teach vary in size, so they might not even know who you are.

It is important to keep in mind that with courses with large class sizes or at large universities, faculty members often do not care about you (as an individual) and your success. Remember, unlike high school, there is no one to hold your hand and all success is dependent on you as an adult! Your parents will not be fighting academic battles for you. Students come and go through their courses, and every year, students do well, average, or fail, regardless of challenges or issues. If you want to talk things out, prepare not to receive very much sympathy. However, if there is a human error on an exam or test (the correct answer is marked as wrong), you could always find time to make an appointment or email your argument.

If you get accommodations of any sorts, approach your professors or TAs on the first day. Let them know your situation and get the required paperwork (if any) to them so they know what accommodations you are receiving. They will probably remember you and be able to help you more than if they did not know.

Distance/online learning

I put distance learning and online coursework in the same category because they pretty much go hand in hand, but I want to make the small differences clear. Distance learning is education that you can pursue from anywhere, usually online. It means you can take a class at your university from anywhere in the world with no issue. Online classes typically fit this distance learning mold, but sometimes for an online class it is necessary to be on campus in the instances of group projects, the occasional assignment that might get turned in face-to-face, or an in-person exam.

There are often many advantages to an online class. Typically, you do not physically have to go to a lecture, so if a large crowd scares you, it shouldn't be a problem. If an online class has lectures, they are usually pre-recorded videos. You can listen in your room and with headphones so all you hear is just the lecturer. This also means that if you want to take notes, you can rewind or pause so you don't miss anything. You can also watch the lecture multiple times if you don't understand something, or skip straight to the difficult concepts.

The other thing with online classes is the test formats might be different. Some classes require that you physically take a test with all the other students. Others give you an online, timed test that is open-book (but typically you don't get enough time typically to just skim the book and look for the answers). However, with an open-book test, you should thoroughly check the policy to make sure this means class materials only. I would hate to see you get in trouble for cheating because you were looking for the answers on Google while on campus Internet (they can track these things!). Some classes also require you to install special software to track what you are doing online while taking the test, to disable cheating through web searches on Google or other tabs. Remember though, if you do these things thinking "no one will catch you," there is always the chance you will get caught, and if you just Google everything, you are not learning! The idea of class is to learn!

However, when in an online class, you should still treat it like a regular class. Choose a few times a week to have "class-time," where you either work on writing assignments, taking tests or quizzes, reading the textbooks, or watching lectures. Make sure to read the syllabus very clearly to see when the due dates are. Due dates are very firm in online courses since the class is available to you 24/7, and you have lots of time to work on things. Make sure to put every due date on your own calendar so you don't miss anything. Some classes are self-paced where, as long as you finish by the end of the semester, it's no big deal, but make sure to stay on a schedule for those so you don't end up doing an entire course during finals week!

Grades/grade point average

Every class you take will have a different grading scale, and that grading scale is dependent on the amount of assignments, exams, quizzes, and difficulty of the course. From my experience thus far, an "A" could be anywhere from an 87 to a 95, depending on the course. Sometimes, grades are firm and other times they are not, but you can find this out in the syllabus. If grades are not firm, the instructor can apply a curve at the end of the semester. A curve will never hurt you—it can only bring your grade up, and be the different between an "A" and a "B," or a "C+" or a "B−."

Each letter grade you receive contributes to your GPA. A high GPA is important if you are trying to receive honors for your work each semester through the Dean's List, or want to eventually graduate with Latin honors such as cum laude. The higher your GPA, the better honors you will get on your transcript and at graduation. These transcript honors are given to employers after you graduate, and will have them note that you are an exceptional student.

If your grades are good, you will also have more doors open to you. You might get more offers for internships, TA roles, or invitations to prestigious honor societies that are either worldwide or nationwide, such as the Golden Key International Honour Society (www.goldenkey.org) and Phi Beta Kappa.

If your grades are bad, you might be on probation with the university, or restricted from certain activities. Some clubs and organizations require a certain GPA, and so do some programs for you to graduate. If your grades are low, talk to an advisor about easier classes, a counselor for emotional help, or drop or withdraw from difficult courses so your grades and GPA are higher.

Exams

I hate to be the bearer of bad news, but you can't treat exams in college like you did in high school. You will not get the results you want if you simply go to class every day or read the textbook. Exams in college like to challenge the way you think and see how creative you are in your approaches. They also like to ask difficult questions to prove you know what you learned as well as have you think critically. It is about understanding and mastery rather than regurgitating information like in high school.

One of the best resources available to you for studying is a file of old exams. Some professors will give you the advantage of allowing you to study from last year's exams with the answer keys, while other old exams you will need to source out yourself from older students, the Internet, paid tutoring services, or a library of old work (via a fraternity or sorority, or a student organization relating to your area of study). Old exams show you the types of questions the professor might ask, and how you need to think. However, not every class has this resource available—usually the popular ones and difficult ones do. Most freshmen classes should have this available so make sure to take advantage of old exams.

Start studying in advance. You should be given all of the exam dates on your syllabus, so there is no excuse for you to "forget" when exams are. I would put all the dates on your calendar once you decide you are definitely not dropping the course so you know when they are.

Academic help and tutoring services

College is not any easier than high school, and cannot be treated as such. No one makes it through college alone without asking questions, reviewing, or getting outside help. If your class has hundreds of students, how can you expect your questions to be answered, let alone heard by your professor or graduate student? Unfortunately, there comes a time and place to ask for help, and college is crawling with opportunities to help you get a better grade in difficult classes.

If you have a question and aren't sure how to answer it during lectures, or while doing the work, write it down. That way, you will remember your question when you find the right person to ask. If it is a simple question about a mistake on a problem or incorrect information, send an email to the professor since that is not an academic question and is a minor thing that can be corrected to help everybody (and many others probably noticed the same things you did, but were too shy to say something!). If your question is more complex than correcting a human or technological error on behalf of the instructor, it is time to start utilizing your resources.

If your question pertains to something that cannot be explained via email, or is a visual type of question (math and sciences tend to have more "visual" explanations), you must seek help in-person. If it is a quick question or a single question, find out when your professor or the TAs have office hours. Office hours are walk-in times when you can ask your professors or TAs questions and they will help you to the best of their ability. It is best to only have one or two questions as many students use these office hours for different reasons.

If you completely do not understand a concept, your first step should be to look over your notes and see if the lecture is available to you online (some in-person classes record lectures for you to reference or in case you miss class). Try some examples and if you still don't get it, it's time to take more drastic measures.

Your campus might offer free tutoring services, especially in math and science since those are the fields students tend to struggle with the most. If there are free tutoring services available to you, make sure to check them out. They might often hold review sessions or be available to completely teach something to you individually.

However, there are also paid tutoring services. These services can be found at large universities, and have been around for quite some time. Paid tutoring companies employ older and former students who mastered the material and are able to teach it. Paid tutors will basically teach you in their areas of expertise and answer all your questions because, well, you paid them to. I think that paid tutors are usually pretty good since they've been doing it for a while and know certain professor's patterns, teaching styles, and tests so they are able to help you prepare best with years of experience.

Remember, if you ever need anything extra with accommodations, the disability resources are available to you and can always help you get more time on tests, tutors, specialized note-takers, and other valuable tools to help you succeed. They are some of the few people on your campus who *do* care about your successes!

Time management

Time management is the key to success in college and in life. Time management is a recipe of organization, prioritization, and motivation.

The first step is a very important thing you can do in order to manage your time: stay organized. I'm not saying organized as in your room needs to be spotless, because let's face it, mine isn't either, but I consider myself academically organized. Being organized to manage your time means something a little different, and being disorganized isn't being messy as much as it is causing pointless stress in your life. In order to begin staying organized for school, make yourself a schedule. You could write it down and put what times of day each day you're in class, when you plan on studying, showering, doing homework, socializing, sleeping, etc. This might help you stay on track during the days. Another thing you could do (which is really fun sometimes) is make a to-do list for each week. I would handwrite it since that's where the fun comes in. On your to-do list, you'll put down tests, quizzes, essays, homework assignments, meetings, or whatever you have going on that week that is important. As you finish assignments and meetings end, you get to cross them off (the fun part) and have a feeling of accomplishment that you're actually doing something productive. Another thing you could do to stay organized is make a calendar on your computer or your smart phone. This is what I do—I have a Mac, so I use iCal for my scheduling since it also syncs with my iPhone. I put every due date for major assignments and exams, as well as when I plan on going home. I also put the times and dates in for everything too. I get reminders when I log on to my computer the day before something is happening or due, so I will then remember if I have been putting things off. My calendar is not the place for everyday things such as which classes I have, since I don't need reminders to know I have class each day and where I'm going, but I would have a daily reminder for something such as a medication or vitamins so you remember to take them.

Now that you have a calendar, a to-do list, or other form of organization, it is time to move on to the second part of the formula for time management and success: prioritization. Prioritizing is organizing what you are going to do in order of importance and difficulty, as well as being proactive about things. When you're trying to figure out what to do first, think about what is rational. You're most likely not going to take a shower and dry your hair in the middle of the night, and you're not going to eat breakfast late at night. In these examples, you'd have breakfast in the morning and take your shower at a normal time of day when you could take as much time as you need and won't bother your roommate or others who live nearby. You will also rank these basic needs as high importance so you don't go hungry the entire day and are clean, and will be putting them on your everyday schedule. After you address the basics, it is time to begin prioritizing your academic life: if you have an exam to study for, quizzes, essays, and other homework to do, how are you supposed to get it all done? That is where prioritizing comes in handy. You could start with the hardest thing first, and then as you get more comfortable with working, you could get the easy stuff done, or you could do the easy things first to get them out of the way and focus the majority of your time on the consuming and difficult tasks. Plan out how much time you think everything will take (if you know the material for an exam, perhaps writing an essay will take longer than studying or reviewing concepts) and when it is due. Start working on assignments in advance. If it is due late Friday night, do not start the assignment on Thursday or early Friday night. That is procrastinating and you might not even have enough time or feel well enough to do it. Half of being proactive is preparing yourself for the unknown. That means you have no idea what will happen and thus you are getting ready for it. For all you know, you might get invited out to dinner on Friday night. If you got the assignment done, you could go. If you get sick, you might not want to do the assignment or you might need rest, so if you get things done on time and early, you will be able to take better care of yourself. I like to get things done on the weekends or when I know I have time during the week. Writing an essay on the due date is not the way to go. You will not be putting in your best effort when you procrastinate, since you will feel so pressured just to submit something on time that you can't check over your work.

My final piece of time management advice is motivation. If you are unmotivated, you won't have it inside of you to get organized, make a calendar, a to-do list, or even think about what you want to do first. If you feel unmotivated, you could reward yourself for getting things done. I do this all time. If I get an assignment done, I will allow myself a little break to go check Facebook, call my parents, or draw a picture. I do what I have to do before I do what I want to do, and that keeps me going. Trust me, talking to people or wasting time on the Internet is far more interesting and a better use of my time than a history essay. But I know if I don't write a history essay that I'm supposed to, my grades will slip, I'll feel pressured and stressed, and become anxious about getting it done on time, so I'll write it so I can have fun that weekend instead. It is ultimately a balancing act. Reward yourself with something you enjoy, such as playing video games, a nice dinner, dessert, or just extra sleep. Once you have the motivation to manage your time wisely, you will be able to stay organized and begin to attack the tasks you have to do one by one.

Advising

Are you in the middle of exam week and have no idea when to begin scheduling for next semester? Are you in a program you hate? Do you just have no idea when to begin planning for your future? In any of these examples, going to see an advisor is the best thing you can do. Advisors are specially trained individuals on campus that get paid to help you out of these pickles. They can help you with applications for graduate school, scheduling, changing your major, or assessing your interests to help find things you might be interested in.

If you go to a smaller college, you might be assigned an advisor or be seeing the same advisor each time you need to see an advisor. In this case, it is best to know who your point person in advising is, know their name, and be extra friendly and get to know them as well so they can best help you. If you go to a large university like me, you'll end up seeing a few different advisors during your course of study.

When making the decision to see an advisor, check if you need an appointment or if you can walk into an advisor's office when you want to. If you need an appointment, phone the advising office and be polite to whoever answers, or email the advisor or advising office. An advising website might have these answers, or you could just directly email your advisor if you know who you are going to want to meet with. Show up early for your appointment so it doesn't go to someone else, and because it demonstrates you take advising seriously. While waiting for your turn to meet with the advisors, or while making your appointment, think of a list of questions you would like to ask. Write them down or make sure you remember them. Advisors can't answer questions about specific professors or difficulty levels of certain courses, but they can tell you what you should take or have to take for requirements, if you're on track to graduation, or provide additional information about academic programs of study.

Advisors are busier at some times than at others. Advising is usually at its busiest during the drop/add periods when you can change your courses, the beginning of the semester, and the end of the semester. Once the first two weeks pass, advising sort of hits a lull where you are less likely to wait a long time to see somebody to answer your questions.

If you are having a serious life crisis during your college career because you do not believe you can handle the academic coursework, dislike the school, or your career, there is a chance you may be thinking about transferring or dropping out of school. Many students transfer for a variety of reasons—sometimes to be close to home, or because the school is easier, friendlier, or has more support. If you are planning on transferring, meet with an advisor to learn more about the process, securing transcripts to send, and other plans. If dropping out is something you are seriously considering, I advise that you not make that decision in haste. Dropping out happens more often than normally amongst students with autism, so if that is something you are thinking about, please think it through. Talk to your entire "team"—your family, a resource at the disability office, a counselor if needed, and an advisor—about why you feel you can't continue at the university level or want to take time off before starting again. There are many options out there and dropping out may not always be the right answer—perhaps you need a semester off, a different school, a different program, or something else—so meet with a variety of people to help you address how you feel and what is best for your future.

I've only met with an advisor twice: at orientation, and during my freshman spring. Orientation gave us each a registration advisor that was just for orientation. My orientation advisor was super nice, but she normally worked in the music department so I couldn't ask very specific questions about being a psychology major or psychology coursework. The second time I went to an advisor, I did not make an appointment since I didn't think it would be a busy time to see an advisor. I was wrong—I still had to wait about 20 minutes. The advisor I met with was a graduate student who was employed in the office, and who answered my questions about whether it was possible for me to pursue a second major and still graduate on time. She was able to answer questions about how I was doing on track with my current major (psychology), and how that would affect my progress if I pursued another major. She also wrote down a list of classes I would need to take or choose from, and even told me which ones were the most popular that she saw people with that major take. I have her business card and email, so if I ever want to contact her with more questions, I can.

CHAPTER 5

PROFESSIONAL DEVELOPMENT
CAREER PREP, INVOLVEMENT, AND MORE!

Let me start by saying how much I really hate the term "professional development." It is a term that my university enjoys using for course names, services, and seminars. It is a fancy way to say, "Improve your resumé and become employable." I'm using it because it's a much shorter term, and is pretty concise and somewhat straight to the point.

But unfortunately, the fancy term isn't just some fluff made up by university officials to tell you to care about yourself and provide a reason to pursue ego boosts.

This entire chapter is dedicated to how to make employers want you, how to have an amazing resumé that intimidates people, and all the tips to make your friends jealous of all the offers of opportunities you get.

Resumé/curriculum vitae

It took me until my second semester to realize that your resumé is possibly one of the most important things you will be working on throughout your college career. Your resumé (or curriculum vitae) is your ticket into job interviews because it shows who you are and what accomplishments you have.

When crafting your resumé document, it is important to make sure it looks professional. Do not use any obnoxious fonts or colors—keep it brief and clean. There are lots of great resumé templates that Microsoft Word has available to you, and you could also use templates from the Internet.

Since you are a freshman, it is okay to put your high school accomplishments on your resumé since there is not much you can highlight about yourself from your first few weeks of college if you are applying for a part-time job right away, or are trying to gain membership into that prestigious student organization you heard so much about. You could list things from high school such as what clubs you were in, a highlight of your leadership in band, your community service, or jobs you previously held. However, as you progress through college, make sure to leave out how you were in charge of something during your junior year of high school since you should have accomplished stuff throughout college later on!

When writing about your responsibilities on a resumé, make sure you make it sound concise and fancy. For instance, if you sent emails as your job, make it sound more efficient and professional than, "I sent emails to club members." Use something like, "Organized mass communication for the organization," because it sounds like you did more than send emails. Do not put more than two or three bullets about each position, unless it was the highlight of your resumé that requires the most time. Put from which years you held it.

Make sure you update your resumé often or, whenever necessary in case you need to hand it out!

Involvement

Your involvement is defined as anything you do outside of a career or job. In college, your involvement is which student organizations you join, which leadership positions you hold, or which types of community service you do. Involvement could also encompass more social organizations, such as a planning committee, or professional ones, such as a pre-health society. If you have an office position (or executive board for larger organizations), make sure to highlight that on your resumé.

There is also the question of if you should get involved with certain things just to put them on your resumé. This is really common throughout college—where students join things they aren't completely passionate about so they can get an executive board position later on to put on their resumé, not because they want to do something. If you want my opinion, it's important to be very involved with a couple things to show commitment on your resumé, and if you are ever asked questions about them, you will sound passionate, genuine, and have lots to say. I recommend checking out multiple organizations to find what you like, and sticking to what you like—if you are dedicated and involved with something you love, the prestigious positions associated with it will come in time!

As far as student organization involvement is concerned, I kept mine minimal because I wanted to commit to several things I felt passionate about for all four years of my experience. I am part of an autism awareness club that also is a nonprofit that benefits the autism community in my college town and does service days as well as student awareness events. After a year with them, I am now on the officer team and work on marketing and publicizing our cause and events. I am also serving on student government to plan events and help disabled students on campus. I chose to be involved primarily with these two things since they are what I am most passionate about, and relate to what I want to do with the rest of my life. I am committed to advocating for those with autism and disabilities, so I thought my involvement outside of class and writing would be best to complement my interests. I do plan on getting a little bit more involved by finding a pre-law organization to join so I can learn more about what I am getting myself into for the future though.

Internships

Internships are work experiences that most times are unpaid, but are very valuable for gaining experience with large companies or specialized fields. Most internships are available to you through your college. Classes that have guest speakers might offer internships, companies that come to career fairs offer internships, or there will be postings throughout social media looking for interns. If you look on social media such as Facebook for an internship, you are most likely to come across marketing internships (no surprise, since it's being marketed to you!), so unless marketing is your field of choice, it is time to search further. Think of a company you like that pertains to your field—for instance, if you are a journalism major, think of a popular magazine or newspaper that you like. Go to their website and see if they have an internship program locally or for during the summer, and if they do, apply for it. You can do this for many companies and see if there is a college program, and if there is, it is an option for you.

If not, there are websites that collect internship postings if you are in college and could help you find your dream internship. Monster College (www.collegemonster.com) and Intern Queen (www.internqueen.com) can help your search.

Also, keep in mind that you know lots of people! You might not be the best of friends, or you might not know them very well at all, but maybe that friend of your parents is looking for an intern in your dream field. It would not hurt to ask that person or have your parents ask since they know them better than you, but it is always an option.

Career fairs might also recruit companies to have a presence at your college, and in those cases, you could hand out resumés hoping an internship comes up. I know a lot of internships that come out of fairs and showcases, so make sure to dress professionally, have resumés on hand, and be friendly if you go to these.

Once you landed your internship after sending in resumés and interviewing, it is your job to live up to the responsibilities. If you do a very good job at your internship, you could get course credit depending on your college, get reference and recommendation letters for future jobs, put the internship on your resumé, or best of all, be offered a permanent job at the company you interned at. The work experience you gain at an internship might help you decide how you feel about your chosen career path, and at the very least, prove to be valuable work experience and help you find out what you want to do!

I did have an internship/work experience of sorts during my freshman spring semester. I was a student ambassador on my campus for a national company, and my role was basically to help sell products and do marketing work on campus. I sent out surveys, posted on social media, all sorts of marketing-related stuff that is doable as a full-time student. The work wasn't tailored specifically to me and it did not keep in mind the limitations of my campus, so I had a very difficult time with my internship. I did not continue with it when given the option to move forward and stick with it for another two semesters (summer and fall), mainly because I found myself more frustrated than not, and I did not feel as if I had the time as well considering what I was committing to for the next year. If you get an internship, I recommend working in one that requires you to physically be somewhere and in which you get face-to-face time with whoever you are working for: everyone I spoke to at the company was in different states, so it was very difficult. I also recommend one that has a structured time schedule since I was required to put in a certain amount of hours for the semester and there was no way to keep track of that, so I often felt lost and confused about how much and what was expected of me.

Employment

While in college, it is up to you and your financial situation if you want to have a part-time job. If having a part-time job is something that interests you or you want out of necessity, see if there is an employment office on campus. The safest jobs for a student who lives at school are on campus, and they also cater to students and when you have class. On campus, you could work in offices, dining halls, marketing jobs, or retail (in bookstores). If you have a car or an easy way to get to an off-campus job, you could consider a job at a store or elsewhere part-time. The pay for student jobs isn't great since you are part-time and still degree seeking, but if you need the money or want the experience, it is an option that allows you to work.

If you have a job, remember to be responsible, go to your job, do your work, and still manage your schoolwork. A job should be like taking an additional class as far as a workload is concerned, and the hours should not lessen the amount of time you have to study or do homework. If your job is interfering, talk to your supervisor or boss, since after all, you were offered a part-time position designed for students to be able to manage these duties.

If you are waiting until after college to get a job, make sure you have an idea of what types of jobs you want to apply for since the job market for college graduates is competitive. Your resumé must be relevant, impressive, concise, and have good grades for starters, and then it will ultimately come down to how you interview.

I never had a "real job" like most high school or college kids. I can't say I ever worked in retail, marketing, or any of the common jobs students hold. The closest thing to a "real job" I've ever held was writing this book. While writing, I make time each day for a certain amounts of hours and keep myself on a schedule so I know how to get it done. I also am given deadlines and give myself mini-deadlines on top of the firm deadlines. Of course, by college standards, this job is a lot easier and more enjoyable. I get to wake up when I want, work where I want, wear what I want, and if I want to take a break without a supervisor breathing down my neck, I can. I've worked on this book early in the morning, late at night, in pajamas, in professional attire, on bus trips, in my bedroom, and on the couch while the TV was in the background; all keeping in mind the deadlines and mental schedule I had. It's a great job and I love it, but in order to keep it similar to a true work experience, I set limits, hours, and goals for myself. In order to be successful in a job, you need discipline, confidence to ask questions, motivation, and a positive attitude because every experience you have will help you grow as a person and help you get closer to what you truly want to do in your life.

Interviews

In most cases, being granted an interview means you passed the first stage of getting the position in question—someone read your resumé and/or application and thought you were qualified enough to meet in person to see if you are a good fit! There are many different types of interviews, and lots of people get nervous at interviews. For a person with autism, an interview brings a lot of unknowns as you can never be 100 percent certain what will be asked of you, and sometimes avoiding a question might be in your favor. In this section I'll explain the different types of interview you may encounter, what to be prepared for, and how to stand out!

Types of interviews

THE GROUP INTERVIEW

The group interview is personally my least favorite of the types of interviews, even though it could be the most fun if you are very open-minded, but it could be very confusing at the same time if you read into it too deeply. You will most likely see group interviews for positions that require multiple interviews, and the group interview is the "weed out" interview that could earn you an individual interview. A group interview usually requires you and the other interviewees to work together to answer questions or solve problems through team-building exercises. In my last group interview, we were divided into smaller groups and were required to build the tallest tower possible out of 100 index cards within several minutes and communicate as a group in order to get it done (some of us were placing index cards, others were folding, and someone was giving instructions). After all of the groups ran out of time, we all came together to talk about the challenges of the activity. The interviewers noted who spoke, who did what kind of work during the activity, and inferred traits about them based on their actions, such as if they were leaders or followers. The goal of a group interview isn't to have the right answers or know how to answer a question. My best advice for the group interview is to try to be assertive and stand out. Try to direct the activity, or if they ask questions, say something profound and wise that the interviewers will remember and write down. The good news about the group interview is that a lot of your nervousness is masked by the activities and the lack of direct questions to you. The interviewers aren't paying as much attention to you directly, so certain things such as what you are wearing don't stand out as much either. My best advice is to go in with an open mind and not much of an idea of what to expect, and be respectful to everyone in your attempts to stand out—don't be obnoxious while trying to control a situation or lead. Lead with grace and kindness, as being likable makes you a better leader and others are more likely to follow you.

The panel interview

Panel interviews are intimidating for a person with autism if you want my opinion. There's only one of you, and in most cases, at least two of them (the interviewers)! Every panel interview I've had has been student-run, so the people interviewing me were older students rather than the adults that typically facilitate individual or group interviews. Being interviewed by your peers may also provide discomfort since peer relations are very difficult, and it seems to become more of a popularity contest or likability contest—I've done multiple panel interviews, and probably got two positions out of them. One of them admitted to me after I was selected that they had a few "equally qualified" candidates, but they simply liked me more than the others, which proves to me that panel interviews are likability contests, so get out your most interesting facts about yourself and get ready to roll.

My biggest issue with panel interviews is that you often notice that you are far more prepared than the panelists interviewing you, even if you didn't rehearse beforehand. In every group interview I have had, at least one of the panel members did not read my submitted resumé or application attached, and they always begin the interview with, "Tell us about yourself," and I freeze up because I don't know what they already know about me based on my previously submitted materials. My first mistake with a panel interview was realizing they didn't read my resumé when they first asked this question and I asked back, "What do you already know about me?" or "What do you want to know?" I don't remember which of those two questions I asked, but they were hinting at me to tell them whatever I wanted. I assumed they knew nothing based on their attitudes, so I ended up sharing some basic facts and the entire interview basically resulted in me reading my resumé from memory since they clearly did not read anything they were given. The best way to handle the unprepared panelist is not to lose your patience or temper like I did silently as I began to recite information they should have known, but to be calm. Tell them some of the basics about yourself if there are other students (your name, your year in school, your major, some involvement if it's super important to you, and an interesting fact about yourself). The interesting fact is probably what is going to stick with them the most, so prepare this ahead of time. I know people who say things like what their favorite animal is and it's something random like an octopus with a reason as silly as they think it would be cool to have eight legs, and interviewers remember who said an octopus was their favorite animal.

INDIVIDUAL INTERVIEW

This is the traditional interview and my personal favorite since it is the easiest to prepare for, and chances are, the interviewer is also prepared. More than likely, this person has read your application and resumé, and they might have even tried to Facebook stalk you. Certain employers and professionals I have spoken to told me the first thing they do is look you up on Facebook so they have an idea of what you look like and what type of person you are, which shows that you always have to be careful and aware of what you and your friends are posting. For an individual interview, all the attention is on you, so it is very important to come prepared, know facts and expectations of the position you are interviewing for, and dress appropriately. It is okay to be nervous because the person interviewing you may also be nervous, especially if it is a student. However, do not tell them you're nervous—the interviewer can read your expressions and body language and see how you feel. Try to sit up straight, and use your hands for talking if you aren't playing with them.

THE SKYPE INTERVIEW

When you have an interview over the Internet, make sure wherever you are looks clean. This isn't typical of other interviews, but if you are interviewing from your own dorm room and the messiness (or your roommate's messiness) is visible on a webcam, it will negatively reflect upon you even if you are perfectly qualified. Dress appropriately, and if you're not sure what to use as a background, just sit on your bed against the wall (maybe elevate your laptop by keeping it on a book so it gives the illusion of you at a desk) so the only background is whatever poster is there, or a blank wall. It's a quick way to hide a mess to the interviewer!

THE PHONE INTERVIEW

Phone interviews are by far the easiest ones as the interviewee because you get to schedule the time, be wherever you want, and dress how you want. Choose somewhere quiet or somewhere where you can talk and not be disturbed. When you are on a phone interview, I recommend being somewhere where it is possible for you to take notes and check the Internet if needed. Make sure you are reachable at the number you provided with your resumé (don't give your home phone number, give your cell phone number) and make sure you either have your phone connected to the charger or fully charged. Everything you say will be judged by your voice or tone of voice, so try your best to answer questions honestly and sound enthusiastic! It is very easy to tell if you sound genuine, so try your best.

Preparing for interviews

Sometimes, you have no idea what an interviewer will ask you when the interview takes place. Most interviews ask very similar questions, such as to tell them about yourself, why you're interested, and what makes you different. Make sure to research the organization or position you are interviewing for so your information is accurate and shows that you took the time to prepare. You also want to look your best, so make sure you look clean, organized, and put together since you only get one chance at a first impression.

Interview etiquette

Always use your manners and be polite when you are being interviewed. Sometimes, a compliment could go a long way. Once, a woman who interviewed me had very interesting nail art and I said I liked it. After the interview, if you have your interviewer's contact information, send them a brief email thanking them for their time and consideration, and say that you look forward to hearing from them. Try to smile lots, and appear friendly. Do not insult or speak rudely to whoever is interviewing you. You want to act as if you will fit in with the work staff while being as natural as possible.

Clothing and dress codes

From the premise of this chapter, it really doesn't seem like clothing is such a big deal, but it always is. Every time I have interviewed for on-campus positions, I receive some sort of email or details over the phone with some buzzwords that tell me what to wear to the interview. When I first got to college, I had no idea how important this whole professional dress thing was. I spent so much time on Google trying to figure out what exactly was "safe" to wear to a casual interview, or how conservative I should be.

When I was serving student government, I was required to be on the other side of a conference room table interviewing possible assistants and other qualified individuals to work with me. In order to help out, the organization gave me an evaluation form to fill out regarding whomever I interviewed. The first item on the list I was supposed to evaluate was their professional style of dress on a scale from one (being the worst) to ten (being the best). This only proves how important dressing properly is!

So, in order to help you guys and girls out, here is what all the different cryptic messages embedded in the dress code mean! Please keep in mind that you may not agree with me, but this guide serves to impress the people who are interviewing you and make them immediately respect you, not to make you feel good about yourself, or for your friends to tell you how breathtakingly handsome you are, or to impress someone on the first date.

If the dress code for an interview or job is not stated, you could always ask. Paying attention to those details and asking sometimes even earns you "brownie points" where the employers or others take note of your attention to detail. If they don't give you a straight answer, I find it better to overdress—it pays respect to whoever is hosting you that day, whether professionally or at a party.

Casual

Casual sounds like the easiest one, but honestly I find it to be the hardest one to figure out as far as professionalism goes. It straddles the line between everyday clothes and business casual (discussed next). In my experience, the only casual interviews I've been to have been group interviews, and in a larger group setting what you wear isn't as important as what you say or do because there are so many of you participating that it is more important to speak up and draw attention to yourself. For this concept of "casual," I recommend going one step above jeans and a t-shirt, and finding a collared t-shirt or something preppy to complement a pair of nice-fitting jeans. Wear a belt with the jeans as well. It just helps you look cleaner.

Business casual

This is where things stop making sense to the average person who has never heard of styles of professional dress. Business casual is considered what most people wear to work on a regular basis, and is much more complicated if you are a girl. For guys, business casual usually means wear a button-down shirt with khaki slacks, or other dress pants, a nice belt, and nice shoes. Ties aren't exactly a necessity in business casual. For a girl, a nice blouse and a skirt would work very well. Always keep the makeup light so it is not overpowering, but I think with the jewelry you could be a little bit more creative to show who you are. I like to think of business casual as the "everyday" office dress code. If you wouldn't wear it to work at an office or you can't see your mom wearing it at an office, it probably isn't cool. The overall "nos" of business casual are jeans, t-shirts, sneakers, sleeveless shirts, sweatpants, or anything that you would wear pretty much when you get out of bed and go somewhere.

Business professional

This is the most formal dress style and is definitely the easiest to accomplish. For guys, this is the simple suit and tie look. Make sure your tie says professional, and isn't goofy with something like piano keys or cartoon characters. A solid color or nice pattern works fine. Many department stores and other adults are very helpful in picking out tasteful suits for young guys. For girls, there are skirt suits and pantsuits, and often you could also do a blazer and skirt with pantyhose. If you're more conservative and things fit you funny (like me), go with a clean, crisp dress. Wear natural looking makeup and simple jewelry: a pair of studs is always the answer. Make sure you look together: straighten or curl your hair, your outfit should flow, and a nice purse might also help you look polished. If you have piercings or tattoos that are visible, try your best to cover up. I find professional somewhat easier because it is very conservative and simple.

Internet presence

I want to give another warning about being classy on social media. Please make sure not to post anything you wouldn't want an employer to see!

If you know that employers are going to be checking your online presence and will take note of what is (or isn't) on your Facebook account or other social networks, take the time to check it yourself. Make sure there is nothing you wouldn't want your parents or grandparents to see, for starters. This means no provocative photos, alcohol in the pictures, swearing in public statuses or comments, or anything that would make your family uncomfortable. A conservative approach to social networking is the safest bet you have. Profile pictures should also be conservative—a nice headshot, or an innocent type picture of you with your friends is acceptable, but nothing that shows nudity, profanity, or alcohol or drug use.

If you are going to look for jobs online, sometimes an Internet presence could help you. Sites like LinkedIn, Monster, and Tyba allow you to search job postings and post resumés as well as make professional connections. LinkedIn is known for adults looking for jobs, but there are certain groups on it that could help you, such as your college's alumni network, or even a student organization.

I recommend having a presence on some of these websites if you know you can manage the profiles and keep them up to date and check often. It might help you find what you want, and whom you know might also work in your favor!

Chapter 6

SOCIAL LIFE AND
SOCIAL ISSUES

Meeting new people

Most freshmen come to college feeling lost and afraid they won't make friends. Luckily for you, you're not the only one who might feel this way—everyone does, so you might as well take advantage of the situation and meet as many people as possible before academics get too tough!

If you are like me and have a lot of difficulty meeting new people as time progresses, become more involved on campus and spend less time in your dorm. Go study in a less quiet part of the library so you see new faces. Spend more time outside. If you don't have headphones in, people think you are also more approachable and easier to talk to.

I will admit that having HFA does make it very difficult to socialize at times, especially in the residence halls and dorms. A lot of the time I am simply exhausted from a day of learning in class, and want "me time" and not to go socialize with others who live nearby. I just want to sit on my bed, listen to music, and relax. However, what I've learned is to be social on your own time if you feel up to it: keep your door wide open, or go study in a common space so you can at least say hello to people so they do not think you are mean or antisocial. I try to stay social enough where I live that people know I live here, and that they think I am a relatively nice person (for instance, sometimes I will ask someone who walks by how their day was). Small talk might not go anywhere but is a quick and easy way to seem friendly while meeting people.

If you want to meet people in a setting that is comfortable for you, take advantage of your special interests. Many of us on the spectrum have a range of interests that are surely covered somewhere on a college campus—from anime to video games, obscure music, and sports. Join a club that covers these interests so then you are automatically forced to socialize with people who have similar interests and you immediately have something to talk about, especially if you're one of those people who is an expert on their subject of interest.

If you are very shy or really are anxious about meeting people, I recommend also joining a club or an organization that has a mentoring program and sign up to be a mentee, and later on, a mentor. That way, you will be able to fill out a form about what you are interested in, and who you are, and typically get paired up with an older student with similar interests who will be there for you as a mentor or an older sibling type. When you are older, you will get to have a mentee to look up to you, so you will make a small "family" while on campus through mutual interests. I recently got a mentor from my pre-law fraternal organization, and she and I have a lot of the same interests and get along very well, so I made a new friend without even having to try very hard to find her!

Making friends

Everybody in college is looking to make friends, so this is your opportunity to shine and try your best to make friends. During the beginning of the fall semester, the workload is still light enough that you have time to have a social life.

I still stand by that it is important to look a certain way, even in college. It really will help you meet people if you look put-together, stylish and friendly, especially in the beginning of school. It is a very visual world, and that is how people will make their first judgments of you. If you look good, people will want to talk to you and approach you, so it will be a lot easier to meet someone.

This is especially great if you are shy. If you aren't sure how to be stylish, look at fashion magazines such as Seventeen, Teen Vogue, and GQ. If you just want to find typically stylish brands and take it from there, Hollister, American Eagle, and other mall stores aimed at teenagers and young adults are also helpful. You could also browse the Internet for ideas on how to dress. You should also have some cool gear relating to your school with the mascot on the clothing for sporting events and just showing overall pride—this is especially common with new students to get them excited. Make sure you are also well groomed: showered, shaved, and looking and smelling presentable. I am not saying you need to look ready to wear a tuxedo or a prom dress, but you need to dress to impress in a casual sense. Girls, this means please make an effort with makeup—it can look natural with nice shadow and liner colors, but please try your best. It really is a visual world, and your first step to friends is at least making a good first visual impression.

The first place where you can easily make friends is your residence hall. Your floor is going to consist of people that you will be neighbors with for the entire school year. If you haven't reached out to or met your roommate yet, please do. Either call them at the number the school provided or email them. I would not quite go Facebook stalking them and messaging them there until you've at least spoken so it doesn't seem creepy. Your roommate could end up being a very good friend if you get lucky. Be enthusiastic, friendly, smiley, and kind, and you will be off to a great start. Usually, you will get to meet everyone on your floor when your RA has a welcome meeting. The welcome meetings usually involve some basic social icebreakers where you will get to know each other. Common icebreakers include "Me Too," where you share a fact about yourself and if someone else has that in common, they say, "Me too," sharing names, majors and interests, or being assigned a random conversation partner for several minutes. You might make some new friends out of these icebreakers. I also recommend hanging around common spaces in your building so you see and meet new people.

Your entire residence hall might also have welcome events planned by the residential social committee. These events might be themed, buffet style, or have anything in order to attract residents and get them to meet each other. If the welcome event advertises free food, you should probably go since many students refuse to pass up free food.

My residence hall had at least three events a week during the beginning of the fall semester. On my first night when I moved in, I went to a themed casino night. If you didn't know how to play poker or blackjack, an older student would be your buddy and show you how to play. The girl who lived next door to me also went and we began to talk a lot after the event. Everyone else who was at my blackjack table that night was very friendly, and I talked to nearly everyone. I didn't make friends with each person, but if I ever see them around campus or my residence hall, I wave and say hello and make small talk as best I can. You might not meet your best friend at a welcome event, but you will definitely meet people and make a friend.

The next place you could make a friend is in class. If you have class in a large lecture hall, sit next to somebody random. Say hello to whoever is next to you. You could ask a question like, "What is your major?" or something generic; especially since large lecture classes are usually common for freshmen and have people on many different educational paths. I found asking about majors came in handy mainly in my first math class in college because a lot of majors required pre-calculus at the time. I got to exchange phone numbers and information saying that maybe we could get lunch after class or study together sometime, although I never really followed through and neither did the people I spoke with.

While on the subject of meeting people and making friends in class, you could also form or join study groups, regardless of the class difficulty. Study groups are an opportunity for you to meet socially with a group of people each week on neutral ground (that way you do not have to host anyone or have roommate conflict about having people over). Even though you might be spending most of your time in a study group actually studying, there are still opportunities to make friendships by inviting people to do something afterwards, having a meal together, or quizzing each other one-on-one. Hopefully, after your class ends you will still remain in contact.

Join a club or a sport that you have an interest in. If you used to be a varsity athlete, join an informal sports team so you will get to keep playing and make friends on the team and see others at practice. If you aren't an athlete (like me), join some student organizations that cater to your interests. If one doesn't exist, you could start a new club and attract new members with similar interests. I've met so many nice people through clubs, and it is so nice to know that at least we have one thing in common. Go to all of the meetings and stick around for a few extra minutes to socialize once club business is done. I also recommend going on the service trips or community service days if a club offers those since you will get to help the community and meet and befriend new people through those experiences.

Prejudice

It still pains me to say that the most prejudice I have ever seen and experienced in my life was during my freshman year. I've seen prejudice personally because of my religion and my autism diagnosis. I believe I was discriminated against in certain situations simply because I disclosed I had autism. In others, I know people treated me differently because of my religious beliefs. It's very sad, but you might be discriminated against if you disclose too openly, are a minority, or something else that sets you apart from the "norm."

I used to think that education is the best way to combat prejudice, but unfortunately I don't think that's always the case. We can't educate every person we see about autism and how it affects each of us as an individual. I am writing this mainly as an awareness section. You might experience prejudice or be turned away from certain opportunities if you do disclose your autism simply because someone does not understand or does not want the liability of something happening that they are unprepared for. However, if you have the chance, try your best to advocate for yourself and do your best to educate and inform if necessary. As I mentioned previously, disclose as necessary or if you don't believe it could harm you in the situation.

Student organizations

Joining student organizations and clubs is a great way to get to explore your interests and meet new people with those similar interests. When looking for student organizations to join, find things that you identify with and where you would enjoy getting to meet similar people. There are interest-based organizations, cultural and religious organizations, service organizations, and professional-based organizations. If you feel passionate about a certain interest of yours, see if there is a club that specializes in that. If there isn't, you could form your own club.

Remember to try not to join too many clubs. See what the time commitments are so you do have the time for each club

On top of regular meetings, many clubs have social events in which you go to a restaurant, somebody's house, or a certain place on campus. At these events, many people go to talk to friends or make new ones. I recommend going to a social so you do get to talk to someone new, and if you feel uncomfortable, you can leave eventually.

Greek life (fraternities and sororities)

If you are on a large campus in the US, Greek life probably has a large presence. The Greek system is not the majority of students, although sometimes it seems that way, but student members have a lot of control over the social scene as well as campus politics at many universities. Many men join fraternities and women join sororities so they can make friends, meet people, and have fun as part of a group. Greek organizations all have Greek letters naming them and are part of a national organization; the organization on your campus is a chapter of the larger organization. If you are a member of a fraternity, you're a brother, and a sister if you're a member of a sorority.

If you want to join a Greek life organization, you will have to attend recruitment (rush) events. If rush is something that interests you, check your university's Greek life office or the fraternity or sorority governing body websites. Fraternity rush is different from sorority rush, and at the end, you could be offered an invitation, or bid, to join the organization. If you plan on pledging, or accepting a bid, make sure to consider the costs, time commitments, and ask important questions about issues such as hazing. Hazing is illegal in nearly every organization, but that does not mean it never happens. Hazing is defined as forcing you to do something humiliating or against your will. If you are ever hazed in any organization, report it to a hazing hotline and to your university's Dean's office.

Greek organizations also have many parties and social functions. They often pair up with other fraternities and sororities for homecoming, formal events, philanthropic events, and sporting event tailgates. If you do not feel comfortable partying or going to these types of events, Greek life may not be for you.

A lot of people make friends and connections through the Greek system. Every person in one of these organizations gets an older member as a mentor, known as a "big." A big is supposed to be a friend and mentor to you, and is your connection into the organization. You also meet other people you pledge alongside, so it is very easy to meet different members since most social fraternities and sororities are large and have many members. Also, if you like the people you meet, you might get to live in the chapter's house the next year with your new friends! You might also make friends with similar majors, and have access to old notes and test through the chapter's study room or older members.

I went through informal sorority rush (there is formal and informal rush; formal is when most women join but informal is held for interested women and chapters that don't have full membership at the moment). I decided to learn more about the system so I could have an educated opinion, and I also really wanted to write about it since it is very social and surely difficult for someone with autism. However, informal rush at my university was structured much like formal, except it was one day instead of an entire week.

During rush, it is very important to look good with full makeup, a nice sundress (if it's summertime or a hot spring like it is in Florida), and good shoes that you can take off while walking from house to house for comfort. You want to make an impression so the sorority sisters remember you when they are rushing hundreds of different girls. If you want ideas of what to wear, Pinterest is a great place to get ideas.

Rush is very stressful not because it is important to look good, but because you are having so many conversations with people you don't know. It made for hours of awkward small talk with girls, and I tried my best not to be too nervous (even though I totally was) and to let the conversations flow. If I was lucky, someone I spoke to was from my area back home so we would talk about what we liked best about home or whether we knew the same people. I liked some sisters far more than others at each chapter, and some of them I felt I could have been friends with, while with others I thought we were way too different to be friends.

However, when I went through rush, I was really proud and excited since I was working on this book and at times even shared that with the sorority sisters who rushed me. Some of them were more than impressed. It caused me to mention my autism and I'm not sure how well that was taken. But, I do know my name was remembered because when I ran into a random sorority sister or two on campus, they knew who I was because their sister who rushed me talked about me. By the end of rush, I felt pretty confident in who I was, and at the end, I guess I learned a lot of awkward small talk skills even though I did not think sorority life was for me at the time.

My opinion: if you have autism, Greek life is probably too social. Rush is very overwhelming, but if you go through the process, you might make some friends with other people rushing. The most important thing I learned from my one day of rush was social skills. I learned how to find common ground and have conversations with complete strangers, so I think it made for great conversational practice and it could really help you too if you want to learn.

Outside of the social fraternities and sororities that have houses on campus or the multicultural Greek organizations, there are also professional co-ed fraternities. These national fraternities have Greek letters in their names, but instead of being social or providing a place to live, they are career oriented and professionally driven. These fraternities can provide job and internship opportunities, tips for courses, professors, and mentoring. Like social fraternities, they have a big-little system for mentoring, different socials to meet the other members, but nothing too formal or bigger parties. This might be more for you since it is less of a time commitment and great for learning more about your chosen field of study.

Dating, sex, and relationships

Dating in college is far different than in high school. You most likely do not live at home, have your parents watching and questioning everything you do, and you also have more freedom about where you can go on dates. You also aren't going to be followed by whatever reputation you had in high school.

If you're wondering where to meet people that you might be attracted to, check out the section on meeting new people. I didn't talk much about parties as a way to meet people since most relationships that come out of parties are hookups, one night stands, and often the people are not sober, so you can't tell what they are like normally.

I will once again reiterate my point about looking good. Once again, it is important to be well groomed and keep up with your appearance. Most attraction is initially based on what you physically look like, and if you're too shy to approach people, this is your best bet once you are out of your dorm room. If you look good, you appear confident, and many people are attracted to confidence.

Just looking good and getting out of my room offered me lots of dates. I've been asked out in the library, renting a vacuum at my dorm, on a bus, and by guys I went on retreats with. Keep in mind, I'd been asked out twice in my entire four years of high school, and I've gotten asked out at least four times in one semester. That's proof that whoever or whatever you were in high school has no application to who you are in college. Learn from me: the more you are out and about, the more people will be able to notice you.

Dating in college takes up a lot of time. If you do not feel that you have the time necessary to commit to a relationship, then be polite but honest about your concerns. It is a lot of work to be on the autism spectrum, live independently, and keep up your grades and be a good student, and having a partner might make that already existing workload overwhelming.

When dating, it is important to have trust. You will want whoever you are with to understand what makes you unique, and to be there for you. If you feel the time is right, I think it is important to disclose your autism if you are planning on getting serious about the person you might be dating. You want to be in this together, and the right person will still be attracted to you and enjoy your company regardless.

For all of you girls out there, I know there is often pressure to be in a relationship or to move further into a sexual relationship because of pressure. I want to let you know that you are the boss of you: no other person can tell you what you should and shouldn't be doing, and if you feel uncomfortable about any sexual act or relationship, you have the power to say "NO!" and do what makes you happy!

You might have heard me mention "one night stands" and "hookups" several times when referring to parties and other places with alcohol. These all refer to sexual relationships that are very temporary. I'm hoping you had a sex education class in high school, so you probably know about all of the different aspects and consequences of these relationships, such as pregnancies, sexually transmitted diseases (STDs), and feelings regarding respect and self-esteem. If you are planning on having sex, whether it is with a temporary partner or you are in a committed relationship, please be safe and be on birth control, use condoms, or be ready to handle any consequences.

If you are planning on being sexually active, make sure to check out the on-campus healthcare available to you. Campuses might offer low-cost birth control pills for women and free condoms for anyone who needs them, so take advantage. Student healthcare also has screenings for STDs and pregnancy tests at a low cost as well, so if you are feeling unsure about a decision made or just want to make sure you're safe, make sure to go. Do your research on the health website for your school to see what is available to you. There are also vaccines against certain diseases that are transmitted through sex or to which your susceptibility increases with sex, such as HPV and cervical cancer, that you could get vaccinated for while on campus, so make sure to take advantage of what you can get because it will more than likely be cheaper for you at school than at home. If you aren't planning on being sexually active in college, I would get vaccinated anyways since you still can, and it will lower your risks for the future of certain diseases you surely don't want to ever end up getting.

Nightlife and parties

I would be lying if I denied the existence of the party scene and nightlife in college towns or near universities. If you know where to look, there are parties or people willing to party every single night, no matter what day of the week it is or which classes or exams are the next day.

Most nightlife in college involves drinking at pubs and bars and going to nightclubs or house parties. If you are under 21, keep in mind that underage drinking is illegal. Police officers break parties up fairly often, and you do not want to get in legal trouble for underage drinking. Parties are usually very noisy with lots of people intoxicated and might be far from your dorm. It could be a stressful situation, especially if you go with friends who drink. You might be the designated driver for those who can't get home themselves, responsible for calling a cab, or making sure they don't get taken advantage of. Many people at parties go simply for hookups—meaning, they want sexual encounters while drunk. They aren't usually looking for relationships.

Nightclubs are also an option for nightlife other than parties and bars. Nightclubs do serve alcohol, but depending on the club, you might be allowed in if you are 18. These places do their best to prevent underage drinking by making sure of who is allowed to drink and who isn't upon paying cover charges (or entrance fees). If you go to a nightclub, go with a group of friends so you don't get approached by too many strangers who may want to dance or drink. The music is loud in nightclubs and it is very difficult to have a conversation, but there are usually sitting areas where you can rest for a little while, although it will still be pretty loud. As usual, always go in a group so you don't have to walk alone anywhere at night and you can look out for each other. Sometimes, the nightclub promoters like to take pictures of all the action that night and post the photos to their Facebook pages. If you don't want them to take a picture of you and your friends, tell the photographer before they snap a picture, or make sure you don't look under the influence regardless of whether you are—these are the types of photos that could haunt you! If a nightclub photo of you does surface on the Facebook page, send the club a message to remove the picture so it is not online for eternity.

I have only been to one house party and never went to any fraternity parties. I don't want the risk of the police breaking it up, don't want to be around too many drunks, and I don't have a responsible friend to go with. When I did go to the house party, I had a friend go with me. He said if I felt uncomfortable at any point, we could leave, which gave me peace of mind while I tried socializing with strangers. It did end up getting uncomfortable for me, and he stuck to his word and took me home afterwards. I have also been to one of the more indie-style nightclubs a few times. I learned with nightclubs if you go early, it is a lot quieter. If you wait about an hour or two after opening, it tends to get louder and the dance floor becomes full of people and wall-to-wall, so if you have personal space issues, I would go early and leave early. I've been to a club early, and I've been during the middle of all of the action on the dance floor. I will never go alone; I will always go with at least one friend. What we do is we have an exit strategy before arriving: we set a leaving time the second we walk in (no later than about 1am). The leaving time guarantees we'll get home at a decent hour, get sleep if we have a class in the morning, and won't be stumbling out at the same time the drunken crowd does. I try to time my club exposure to about an hour or an hour and a half at a time. It is all about planning, getting to and from safely, and being responsible. For instance, every time I have been to a nightclub was after a very stressful exam so I wouldn't think about how I'd done, or if my class the next morning was cancelled (I've only been during the week because I believed it would be less crowded and the theme nights were better). Just stay safe and be responsible!

Nightclubs and parties both have a common theme of being crowded and loud. When I went to the party that time, I had an agreement with a sober friend about taking me home when it became too much. A lot of the noise was also concentrated around the kitchen area, so I went to the living room to sit down and recollect my thoughts since it was quieter. Nightclubs are usually louder than house parties and finding a quiet place can be harder. Sometimes they might have bright lights and other things that could make you react differently. If you are looking for somewhere to go to recollect your thoughts in a quieter place at a club, I recommend going to the bathroom actually to "cool down" from being around so many people and the noise, because it is usually quieter there. This is true especially if you're a girl, since girls are usually in the bathrooms in order to fix their makeup or because they are sick from drinking too much alcohol. As always, if it is too much to handle, you can leave at any time. It is important to know what you can and can't handle, and if you have a responsible buddy to go with, they will absolutely understand that you feel as if you need to leave.

Weekends

After a full five days of class, studying, exams, and quizzes, you are happy to realize the weekend is finally here. On weekends, you can sleep as late as you want, do whatever you want, etc. There is a lot of free time in college, and weekends are just the beginning. There are activities like nightlife, sporting events, large-scale student charity events, or just hanging out. Weekends are a great time to catch up with friends and family, or if it's feasible, to go home. However, you might also be studying for midterms, sleeping, relaxing, or other things.

I find the thing with weekends is you tend to have a lot of "down time," but you're still expected to be smart about it. As far as weekends go, I recommend you still stick to a schedule since you could probably get bored very easily if sporting events, partying, and socializing are not activities you want to take part in and you don't have the option to go home. Make sure you're awake by a certain time (I usually like to give myself until 10 am or 11 am so I can catch up on much-needed and wanted sleep), shower, and be dressed. That way, if you have plans unexpectedly, you are ready to go somewhere or see people other than your roommate.

I use weekends primarily to study and get ahead so I am less stressed during the week and I am distracted from thinking about my lack of social life. If you are enrolled in a paced online class, meaning you have deadlines each week, I'd recommend you get ahead for the next week or finish up the previous week if you haven't had the time to do so. If you have a paper due, get started on thinking about what you want to write about, or begin writing the paper. If you have an exam, study. If you have homework, do it over the weekend. By getting ahead, you can have more fun during the week or use the time more effectively to study, go to a club meeting, see a friend, go to an on-campus event, or something else that seems like time well spent to you.

It would also give you time to review your work, such as revising your essay, checking your answers on homework, or giving you extra time to study.

Sporting events

I go to a university with over 50,000 students. The seasons and times of year on our campus are measured in sporting seasons. Which sporting events your school has might depend on its size. The reason sports are so popular on my campus isn't the fact that our programs are widely funded, but it brings all 50,000 students as well as countless alumni and fans together for a day at a time. Sporting events usually come with a bunch of activities. One of the most popular sporting event pregame activities is tailgating. Tailgating is usually just making barbeque food, flipping burgers, drinking alcohol (if you're legal), and having fun with a group before the game. Home games (which are on your campus, or in the town depending on which arenas and facilities are nearby) are the local ones that usually do have tailgates and students attend. These arenas can be packed with thousands of students and be very loud, so if you wouldn't enjoy being around so many people, you can always just watch the game somewhere else, like a sports grille restaurant or at home on television. Either way, if sports are a big deal where you are, you should at least know who is playing and who wins the game. I recommend at least trying to go to one sporting event just to say you have done it for the experience.

I've only been to two types of sporting events: football and basketball. Football is huge on my campus; our stadium seats close to 90,000 people. As a student, going to a game is very accessible because students are always selling tickets, and before the season begins we get access to cheap season tickets. I went to my first football game very nervous and with a large group from my dorm so I would feel a part of it. I didn't watch football at home, I barely knew the rules, I didn't tailgate or anything: I simply wanted to know what the big deal was. I wore my school colors with pride and remember nearly passing out from standing in the September sun. Some girl in my football ticket group got me a water and I couldn't have been more thankful since I really was about to pass out from dehydration that day. What I learned is, no matter what, go buy from the concession line at the beginning of the game before it gets too crowded and monitor yourself. After that, I expected to be incredibly tired from standing for hours (our campus culture is students never actually sit down during the game, unless it is halftime or a commercial break for TV), but I never felt so excited. The feeling of a touchdown sent 90,000 people into hysterical cheering. When I went to the football game for the first time, I felt a part of my campus and a part of something bigger than myself. It was exactly what made me love where I went to school for the first time—the overwhelming spirit.

However, I didn't quite have the same exciting experiences during basketball season. I expected basketball to be really fun in person. I love watching the Miami Heat on TV, so I figured I would feel the same watching my college team. The arena was full since I chose to go to my first basketball game when we were playing a nationally ranked team because I figured it would be a better game. I thought nothing would be louder and rowdier than football; I was told that basketball is fairly quiet since it's during the week, it's indoors, and there aren't tailgates and as many drunken fans stumbling in. I was sorely mistaken. The acoustics of the arena made everything echo a certain way, so everything turned out to be much louder than it actually was. My ears were ringing worse than at a rock concert. I was anxious. I asked my friend at halftime if we could leave, even though the game was pretty good. I was experiencing the typical autism sensory overload. It happens to me sometimes, and I really thought if it was going to happen, it'd be at a nightclub or a football game, but I was wrong. We left the basketball game and laughed it off and swore to each other never to go again.

Sporting events are almost always loud and hard for someone with autism. Some sports, however, are quieter than others, so those might be a better fit. Baseball in particular is typically quiet since the arenas aren't as large as football or basketball, not as many people go to the games, and the season is during a busy time of the semester usually. You could always suggest going to a less popular sport if your school offers those, or go to a club or intramural game since those are less populated but still have a similar experience of watching your fellow students compete. You could always make up an excuse to leave early, such as you want to beat the crowds home (this works especially well in larger sporting events), you have work to finish, or you forgot to do something and you won't remember later. It really depends on who you are with. Leaving is especially acceptable if your school's teams are performing very well or very poorly in the game so you already know who wins pretty much, so that's another good reason to get out if you're lucky enough to have a game that's far from close.

Social media

When I began writing my first book nearly five years ago, social media was sort of a new thing and I would caution against my peers having it. But, that was middle school. In college, you should know the basics of online safety after surviving high school. I'm not worried about college students giving out too much personal information and having the same issues a middle or high school student would.

I've met so many different people in college and can't name one person who doesn't have a Facebook account. Everyone, with the exception of one person from my high school graduating class of over 200, has Facebook. I'll be honest: Facebook is great. I find out about nearly every on-campus organization, contact, and event through Facebook since it is such a popular way to learn on a college campus. I'm also a member of study groups and groups for certain courses where we try to answer questions for each other. However, with this great advantage in your college career, comes the important thing: be responsible. Facebook should be looked at as a privilege, and with that, comes responsibility. Do not post or allow your friends to tag you in anything degrading, try not to swear online, or do anything you wouldn't want your parents to see. I caution you about responsibility because anything you put on the Internet is permanent. Even if you delete it, Facebook stores it and it's still accessible if you're smart enough to look in the right places.

Responsibility is also important when it comes to other social media outlets such as Twitter, Instagram, Vine, and Snapchat. You might think things get deleted instantly (as Snapchat claims), but things stay on servers or in cyberspace forever. These more concise, image-based social outlets are very important to be responsible on since people often post videos of their drunkenness, stupid behavior, sexy outfits, etc. Anything you post on social media could be seen by nearly anyone. Employers often try to get an impression of you before an interview based on your Facebook, so do not post anything provocative, overly political, or anything that could offend or cause controversy. I find it is easier to say very little online and be more of an observer, and only post when necessary (for instance, when I advertise an event I am hosting on campus, or am sharing a huge accomplishment).

Drinking, drugs, etc.

Drinking, drugs, and illegal substances are rampant on college campuses. You might even get offered something that makes you feel uncomfortable. You might just know it's there and never see it. Either way, somehow, this equation affects you.

As I mentioned, in many social activities alcohol is served and used to get people excited, loosened up, and more willing to do things they normally wouldn't. The legal drinking age depends on where you live. If you are under that age (typically 21 in the US), you could get into trouble for underage drinking. There are also many other consequences to drinking too much, such as blackouts, hangovers, and alcohol poisoning. If you have a drinking problem or know a friend who does, utilize the resources campus counseling gives you or something like Alcoholics Anonymous. Also, if you are under the influence and not home, call a cab or have an action plan for a designated driver so there are no drink-driving accidents.

Drug abuse is also common in college, whether it be smoking marijuana or abusing prescriptions. The most shocking thing that happened to me regarding drugs is someone asked me on a camping retreat if I take Adderall—a brand ADHD medication that would be abused in order to concentrate and stay awake. I asked why, and they had assumed I would because of my autism and offered me a deal to sell it to them. I do not take this medication, and if I did, I would not sell it. You would be surprised at the kinds of lengths people go to in order to get drugs like that, and if you are offered to sell your medication to anyone, even if it is a legal prescription from your doctor, do not sell it! There was a case in the news recently about a Californian high school kid with autism who was asked to get his new friend drugs, and when he did, he was arrested because his "friend" was an undercover cop who targeted the kid's special needs and desire to make friends.[1] Do not allow yourself to be taken advantage of, and know that whatever medication is given to you is for your use only as prescribed by your doctor!

When it comes to drinking and drugs, please make smart choices and be aware of anything fishy!

---

1   See http://abcnews.go.com/blogs/headlines/2013/05/parents-claim-calif-school-district-failed-to-protect-autistic-son-in-drug-sting/ for details.

CHAPTER 7

STRESS AND MENTAL HEALTH

College is an emotional rollercoaster sometimes, and pretty much every student goes through different issues throughout their first year. However, these might be magnified by an autism diagnosis. It is now time to tackle all the major plagues that might get in the way of a fun, happy, and successful year.

Homesickness

With living away, one of the most common things freshmen students face is feeling homesick. You miss being home. You miss your pets, your family, your old life, having a more consistent routine—all the great things about being home. You might cry, ask to go home, want to transfer, and be overcome with emotions when it comes to wanting to go home. I know I've been homesick many different times during my college experience, especially the last week of spring semester. My friend remembers me crying about how much I hated our college town, I was bored, and I just wanted to go home after seven weeks away (the longest stretch away from home I'd had all year).

If you feel homesick, it is okay. It is normal for you to feel homesick. Don't be afraid to call home, talk to someone, or find a way for your family to visit you or to go back home. Your family will always support you, and they miss you and worry about you too.

Stress, anxiety, and feeling overwhelmed

As a student with HFA, I can say I am constantly stressed in some capacity and I easily feel overwhelmed. When you feel stressed or overwhelmed, it is important to make time for yourself to chill out. Being too stressed out could lead to a meltdown, or you might actually get sick because of your compromised immune system. It's very easy to end up feeling this way. Maybe your social life isn't what you wanted. Maybe you have too much homework. Maybe you want to go home and you have a big exam and a paper due. Sometimes everything just builds up, you get anxious, and you don't know where to begin gathering your thoughts. This happens to me on a regular basis. Heck, I even chose to address this topic at a time where I felt overwhelmed between schoolwork, writing this book, and so many other commitments I had because it felt more than appropriate to write it at the time!

When you feel overwhelmed or stress, take a deep breath. Think about what is overwhelming you. Is it your workload? The people around you? Something else? Once you decide what is bothering you, think about how you would be able to reduce that stress. Will it go away once you get it done, such as taking an exam, or do you have to think beyond that? Once you decide on a game plan, it's time to tackle things head on.

If you're feeling stressed, don't get yourself down on negativity. Everybody gets stressed. It is okay to feel overwhelmed. Sometimes, it's okay to cry or overreact because you're anxious about being away or you just don't feel right. You owe it to yourself to relax a little bit. If you live in an apartment, take a bath. Take a walk, listen to calming music, or have some fun playing a game or doing something mindless so you don't have to think about why you're stressed, and then you'll feel recharged and able to tackle what's in front of you with a clear head.

Feeling lost

When you're new to a campus, don't know anybody, and don't know where to begin getting involved or what you want to do with your life, it's very easy to feel lost. Maybe you're so confused you want to transfer or just curl up into a ball and go through the motions and then figure out your life. It's not the blues, and might be nerve-wracking, but you might just simply feel lost in such a scary, new place.

If you feel lost, it's time to evaluate why. Did you not meet as many people as you had hoped? Are there just too many cool things to do? Do you have no idea which major is right for you, or just miss home? Maybe it is time to figure out your goals. Think about yourself and what you mainly want to accomplish in college as well as what interests you. Check websites to see what happens on campus, if there are any clubs pertaining to what you enjoy, and if you could meet with someone to talk about what you would like and they could help you find your way (usually someone in career services or an involvement chairperson).

Depression

If you don't want to ever leave your room, can't sleep, are crying, and just losing interest in what you love and your appetite is changing, you might be depressed. If you feel depressed, it is important to know it might not just be a phase. A lot of college students report depression during their first year. The most important thing you could do, according to every psychology class and speaker I've heard, is to seek help. Don't be embarrassed. There are many options, such as talking to someone, therapy, and medications.

Your diagnosis

I feel like a friend to you, we've talked so much about who to disclose to, who to meet, and different survival tips with autism, but we never once mentioned how you feel about it and what it means to you. Autism sounds like one of those words that you might be using to label yourself: you're autistic. But, as your friend, I want you to know you're more than that. Autism might be a new thing to you if you're the kid who just found out about it recently or thought you were different and weren't able to define it. Autism does not define you. I want you to be able to embrace it and know it is a part of you: you might have autism, but it does not have you. It is a piece of your puzzle. You have so many talents and gifts because of your autism.

If you are afraid of your autism or just feel as if you are alone and want some help confronting your diagnosis, see what kinds of autism services are on your campus or in the area. The disability office might have some stuff for you—local nonprofits, support groups, etc. You are definitely not the only one with autism on your campus as the statistics today are about 1 in 80 children—that means in a large lecture class of 500, there are probably four students other than me who have an ASD or are undiagnosed. Surely there is something out there for you.

In the event I haven't convinced you that you are *awesome* for being you, or you still don't feel confident in knowing you have autism, talk to your family. They know you better than I do, and I know they love you and think you're awesome. They might just be able to give you the pep talk you need to continue onward and know to take pride in the "label." If that doesn't work, join a support group to make friends who also are on the spectrum, and talk to a counselor or someone who is more experienced with individuals like you.

Counseling

If any sort of issue is bothering you while you are living away, there are counseling options available to you as a student. Most of them are free or low cost. If you need behavioral or mood-related medications, make sure you either have your old ones from home or meet with a psychiatrist and know of a local pharmacy that would fill them for you.

If you are having serious issues, such as thoughts of suicide, serious depression, or anything else, please call a hotline number so someone will talk to you at any hour of the day and help you out.

CHAPTER 8

LIVING INDEPENDENTLY

Taking care of yourself

If you are not living at home, it is now your job to begin caring for yourself without being reminded what to do constantly, or having someone else help take care of you. Being an adult living on your own means it is your turn to be responsible and take control of your life. With independence, it becomes your job to take care of your needs, advocate for yourself, and be able to survive in your own place without Mom and Dad doing everything for you.

When taking care of yourself, you should map out the different responsibilities you will have. Think about what your parents do on a daily basis: go to work, talk to people on the phone, go grocery shopping, plan meals, etc. These are the types of things that you will be doing, too. If you're not sure how to start doing things, accompany your parents. Go to work with them, or go on a trip to the supermarket to see what they buy. Observation is key and might help things crystallize for you.

Essentially, we can simplify taking care of yourself to: wake up, eat breakfast, shower, get dressed and ready, pack for class, go to class, eat lunch, do homework/study/etc., go grocery shopping if needed, plan dinner, keep working, be social, go to sleep at a reasonable hour, and don't get sick. However, each day does not have the exact same routine. Maybe you want to go grocery shopping on a weekend or go to a sporting event. It really depends but every concept relating to taking care of yourself will be covered in this chapter.

There are certain concepts that you might not think about doing regularly that are important, such as checking your mailbox and getting rid of trash. Unfortunately, these things work differently in dorms than they do in residential areas back home. At home, we have garbage trucks come twice a week and we bring our trashcans and recycling to the curb. At school, I have to empty out my recycling bin and trashcan whenever I get the chance or they are full, by running to a downstairs dumpster and recycling bin. I hate going to the dumpster because I don't like hauling my stuff down two flights of stairs and then walking some, but I know if I don't my room will be a stinky mess and have overflowing garbage. I try to go at least twice a week if I can since I know that is the norm back home. As far as mail, I think it's strange since I never want to check it. I used to believe I didn't get mail. I'm not at camp, my high school friends don't have my address nor did they ask for it, and it just didn't seem important to me, but it actually is! As a student living on campus, I get all sorts of cool mail like coupons, spam for apartment complexes and lease discounts, campus news, honor society invitations, and sometimes the occasional card for a holiday from home. Aside from the actual mailbox, you could get packages, and it is your responsibility to go pick them up, sign for them, or do whatever the protocol where you live is for receiving packages.

Organization

Organization in your everyday life is not the same as being organized to manage your time. I would consider myself super organized when it comes to my schoolwork: I know where all my computer files are, all my due dates are written down, I get reminders the day before major meetings and tests, and I know how to manage what I'm doing, but as far as my living space goes I'm close to a train wreck, especially when I'm stressed and don't feel like I have time.

The first step to being organized so you don't lose things and are aware of where things are is when you're packing to go to college or moving in. I made the suggestion of storage boxes because it keeps my life organized for the most part. Everything for me goes under the bed. All of my medicines and health-related things are in one place, all my electronics are in another, and a lot of random things like socks are all grouped together.

The hardest stuff I find to keep organized is clothing, especially since dorm closets are not exactly large. You also want this to be organized in case you have a roommate and want to make sure nothing goes missing. Anything that is special or normally would not go in the regular wash load in the laundry, I hang up in the closet. Anything hanging is usually a nicer garment, such as dresses, blazers, expensive shirts, skirts, and other clothing items that I know are "dry clean only," "hand wash," or "don't wear unless it's an occasion." Hanging organizers that store clothes are also nice for the closet and those are a good place to keep t-shirts, jeans, leggings, or other lightweight garments so you can hold a lot of them in one spot. I keep one part of the organizer for exercise clothes as well. I also have a hanging jewelry organizer, which I can put all my jewelry in. I would not put all my best jewelry in there since if you are a girl and have a roommate, they might be interested in "borrowing" your stuff, stealing it, or lending it to their friends. Like I said, have a good hiding spot for luxury items and don't keep them in plain view. Nice jewelry is safest on you, actually: my watch, ring, and bracelet from high school graduation are always on my person if I can help it. If for any reason I can't wear my everyday nice jewelry, I have a mini-safe that looks like books, but if you open it to the right spot, there is a compartment for you to store stuff in. It's not high tech or high security, but the books blend in for the most part and I've never taken it out when anyone was around, so it does the trick. For shoes, you could get a shoe rack (I have one at home since I have more space there), or just make sure each shoe is with its mate. If you have a dresser, organize the clothes in there, too. I keep one drawer for socks and undergarments, one for sleepwear, and another for sweatpants and jackets since they otherwise would take up too much room. Always keep socks bunched together—you'd be surprised how many socks I find are missing their mates from being in a crowded drawer or after laundry by not bunching them together.

When it comes to your desk area, you can tackle it in many different ways. Find a place to put all of your textbooks, folders, and notebooks—and designate that area as your spot for them. I also got a paper tray for the upcoming year to put assignments and important documents in so I don't lose them by slamming them into textbooks or random folders. I can pack them right before class, and if I forget and have to run back home, I know exactly where they are. Try not to let your desk become covered in paper. Sort your papers by class into folders, recycle those you know you'll never need again, etc. Clean out old pencils, pens, and everything from inside your desk. I don't do this nearly enough at school or at home, and both my desks have messy drawers and it really doesn't help my situation.

The other point in organization I've noticed is to keep a routine. Many people with autism, including myself, thrive when they have a set routine. I know exactly what times I leave my room for class, when I have class, how long I plan on staying on campus before coming back to my room, and when I have meetings (for instance, one day a week I volunteer so I have that on my calendar). Following a routine and a schedule can help you know when to do certain things, and keep you organized knowing that certain things happen at certain times.

Weather responsibility

"How is the weather?" sounds like the most awkward line in small talk history, right? However, instead of answering it and watching a conversation go dead, or asking it when you have nothing else to say, you'll be asking yourself this every time you wake up in the morning. It is your job to dress appropriately for the weather when you are on your own. You might remember in high school your parents making sure you had an umbrella or a jacket, or telling you to stay dry or warm when you got to school. Now, it is your job to do this.

To figure out how the weather is going to be, you could check your smart phone with apps such as the Weather app, the Weather Channel, or WeatherBug. Local news stations might also have apps specific to your area so you could see if you have weather coming through. If you don't have a smart phone, you could set your location on a service such as Google if you have a Gmail account, or Yahoo if you have a Yahoo account. If your campus has its own television station or radio station, chances are they will also cover the weather on there. Local news also broadcasts weather multiple times per hour as well.

If your college is located in a region that could be impacted by severe weather, such as hurricanes, blizzards, tornadoes, or flooding, you should be paying attention to updates directly from your university. In the event of any natural disaster or severe weather, classes may be cancelled or there will be advisories. If it is too windy, rainy, or anything else that jeopardizes your safety, you should check your email before going to any classes because sometimes the instructor may feel the same way and cancel class.

Now that you are aware of how to check your weather and how to survive the worst weather, it is time to know how to prepare for it. If you know it's going to be cold, dress warmly and if you are extra conservative like me, pack an additional sweater in your backpack or a scarf to keep you warm. I am a true Florida girl and don't know much about snow or even cold weather, but I get cold all the time so I pack a little sweater with me no matter what when I go to class. If it is cold in the mornings but warms up throughout the day, dress in layers. Wear a lighter long-sleeved shirt with jeans and a jacket or two, and as the day goes on and the weather gets warmer, put your jackets back in your dorm or in your backpack so you are still dressed accordingly.

If it is going to rain, do not wear shoes that will either expose your feet to puddles you are apt to trip in, or that could get ruined by the water. This means no flip-flops, sandals, high heels, or suede. Make sure to pack an umbrella too. The larger your umbrella is, the more likely people will approach you to cover them and walk with you if you are alone. This is a great way to make some quick new friends as you shield them from downpours. If you live somewhere where rain is random and common (like Florida), keep a small umbrella or a fold-up one in your bag at all times to prepare for the worst. If you have no umbrella in rain, make sure to take cover, wait it out until it is less stormy and rainy, or "make a run for it" if you aren't likely to slip and are not wearing shoes you'll get hurt in. Your safety is still the most important thing here!

Laundry

If you aren't very coordinated with pouring detergent or aren't good at measuring things, or just want this part of the process to go faster, buy laundry detergent pods. The pods are filled with the proper amount of detergent for one load of laundry and open up once the cycle begins. Looking back now, those are a lifesaver in college since I never have to bring heavy detergent bottles to the laundry room or risk them getting stolen or used by other students. Each washing machine has special cycles for temperature, delicates, lights, and darks. Sort your laundry according to how and when you want everything washed—I put all the light colored things in one pile, the dark (and red) colored things in another, and do additional loads for bedding/sheets, special wash garments that I usually hang to dry, and towels. This also makes choosing the settings easier. The most important thing with laundry, especially in a public laundry room like in a dorm, is timing. Each cycle takes a certain amount of time to wash or dry, and when you start the cycle, put an alarm on your phone or write down the time you need to move your clothes into the dryer or take them home. This is especially important in college because laundry rooms fill up fast and people will move your clothes elsewhere into a pile if you don't pick them up so they can use the machines. Once all your cycles are done, it is your job to fold everything and put them away in your closet, drawers, or elsewhere, and if the clothes aren't going on hangers, you need to fold them. I'm not very good at folding and it took me a while to learn, so ask your parents to show you how they do it because a visual aide is very helpful for this!

Shopping

I bet a lot of girls reading this headline could not be more excited to have an entire section dedicated to shopping. However, this section is not dedicated to the mall, so let's get started by talking about what kinds of shopping you'll be doing in college!

If you're living on your own and are not on a meal plan, or want something more nutritious to eat, you will go grocery shopping. If you are planning to go grocery shopping, you should first plan out how you are going to get there. That is also a determining factor in how much you can buy and bring home with you. If you have a car, or you're going with a friend who has a car, you can bring much more back with you because you can put your items in the back seat or in the trunk of the car. If you are walking, biking, or taking public transportation, you are much more limited by what you can buy. You might want to buy things that aren't heavy and know you are limited to what you can carry with you. To make some more room, I would empty out your backpack from class and use it to hold more stuff—especially if you're buying larger, bulkier things like milk jugs. Before you go food shopping, make a list of what you need or want so you do not get distracted by impulse buys— trust me, the bakery department is really tempting when I have no intention of buying sweets. A list will help you stay on task and avoid those distractions.

When you aren't food shopping, you might also need to look for gifts. Sometimes it might be a family member's birthday, a holiday, or you just need a gift to say "thank you" and do the right thing. This is when going to the mall or bookstore is a good idea. The bookstore has all sorts of cards for birthdays and holidays, and if you want to get stuff that isn't related to your college, it is time to get creative. The mall and other local businesses might be able to help you find the perfect gift for a birthday or family member. Know how to get to these places, or ask a friend which stores are reputable for gifts. Chain shops like Francesca's Collectables, Brighton, Hallmark, and other gift shops might be able to help you.

Online shopping may also be of great service to you. There are lots of discounts available online and certain things for students, too. Amazon sells nearly everything under the sun, and as a student, you will get a free six months of free two-day shipping as well as access to movies and TV shows through Amazon Prime Student. This will help get things that you need ASAP or if you need a rush delivery on something. Make sure when buying brand-name things online that they come from a trusted source so you don't end up with counterfeit goods.

Hygiene

I've mentioned throughout the sections on making friends and meeting people how important it is to look good. Looking good and being presentable and approachable begin at an even more basic level than having stylish clothes and accessories that go with your outfit. Looking good and impressing people (as well as being clean) begin with hygiene.

In college, you don't have your parents to remind you to be a clean, hygienic person. There is nobody telling you when to take a shower, comb your hair, or brush your teeth. This is all now your responsibility and your job. If you have bad hygiene, people will notice. They'll laugh if you have "B.O.," or body odor, and nobody will hang out with you.

The beginning of good hygiene is to set a routine. For instance, you should be showering every day. You could schedule in your brain when you will be showering around how you feel. If you like to shower before class to wake you up in the morning, make sure you set your alarm earlier than normal to account for finishing getting ready and getting to class. If you want to shower between classes, make sure you have enough time to get ready before your next class. If you're like me and like showering after class because of the warm weather or exhaustion, make sure, if you have a community bathroom, that there is a shower available for you to use.

Other than showering and washing your hair, there are other important hygiene things you should know. Whenever you go out, make sure you have deodorant on so you don't stink when you sweat. I would also recommend perfume or cologne to keep you smelling good. Spray enough that you aren't a walking cloud of good smells, but that it keeps stinky smells away and isn't overwhelming.

Girls, you should be wearing makeup. I know makeup is a chore to put on and you might think it's a waste of time. If you're not a huge fan of makeup, at least put it on when you have a class past 8 am or are definitely planning on seeing people you know so you continue to make a good impression. If makeup is not your forte, or you don't know how to apply it, make sure you are reading style magazines since they always have makeup tips. If you need something more visual and faster to learn from, there are many great YouTube beauty channels such as MichellePhan and TheMakeupChair. They will show you how to do all sorts of amazing looks in a short amount of time as well as show and tell you what products to buy.

Always make sure to keep your hair brushed and styled. Guys, this means if you use gel or other products, don't slack off. Girls, this means if you need a blow dryer, straightening iron, or curling iron, use them. Please don't be lazy at the last minute if you have a great outfit and a full face of makeup on!

I am stressing hygiene not because people will compliment you if it's good, but because you will be a bullying target, made fun of, and ignored if your hygiene is bad. I am doing anything I can to tell you how to get off to a good social start and have opportunities opened to you no matter what!

The "freshman 15" and how to avoid it

The "freshman 15" is a nice way of saying that most students who go off to college will gain 15 lbs. in weight during the first year because they are not used to being on their own and typically eat unhealthily. For those of you who think the "freshman 15" is a myth and it won't happen to you, think again. Don't walk in with that attitude, because I did. I thought all the food would be terrible and because of that, I would lose weight. Actually, I gained the "freshman 15" in *one* semester. I am still trying to lose that "freshman 15" and prevent it from happening once again.

I'll tell you exactly how I gained the weight so you can avoid the same pitfalls. First off, like I mentioned throughout the book, it was difficult to go grocery shopping so I never got the proper nutritious things I would need or want, such as fruit. Fruit at the dining hall was typically rotten or didn't look right, so I wouldn't eat it. I normally eat two or three fruits a day, and I was suddenly eating no fruits. I had access to all sorts of junk food through the student union, vending machines, and other on campus eateries, so I would keep emergency candy and goodies in the room. These "emergency" snacks were supposed to be for when I was really hungry, sick, or needed a pick-me-up while studying. Instead, I ate them right away. I also get very stressed and anxious easily because of the pressures of being a college student, so what does a nervous, mildly upset, or depressed girl like me do? She eats junk food to feel better. I'm an emotional eater, and that really doesn't make matters much better. I also used to eat dinner late at night because I had other obligations during the earlier parts of the night, so I would go to sleep on a full stomach, which apparently you are *not* supposed to do. I would also partially blame dating because I would go out to dinner and eat unhealthily fairly often. This, my friends, is how you gain the "freshman 15" in one semester. I knew it was happening simply because I felt my jeans getting tighter, and when I got home, I knew I couldn't keep living this way and feel the need to go buy a new wardrobe to accommodate my expanding waistline.

If you want to avoid the "freshman 15," I'm not saying to eliminate everything I did and that I've done everything wrongly. I know it is perfectly acceptable as a college student to order pizza on a regular basis: it was so regular my freshman year that the delivery driver knew me and would meet me at the back door of my residence hall because he realized it was closer to my room since I would always come out that door to meet him. However, if you can, start a regular eating routine and pretend you're home. Think of what your parents would and would not approve of you eating, and keep that little nagging voice in the back of your head as annoying as it can be.

If your college has one, take advantage of the gym or fitness center. These facilities are either free to students or available at a very low cost, so you might as well take advantage. I know this might sound really weird, especially if you're as athletic as me and got picked last for every team in physical education classes, but going to the gym is helpful to let you eat what you want or keep yourself in shape. Try to find 30-minute intervals on several days a week when you can go walk or run on a treadmill, or do a cardio-type workout to keep your blood pumping and give yourself some energy. It does not matter how athletic you are since very few people pay attention to others working out because everyone focuses on their own workout. If your gym is really high tech, there might be TVs you can watch. If not, I recommend bringing your headphones, iPod, or phone. That way, you can play music while you're running, walking, or doing some type of exercise. If you bring your iPod, make a playlist beforehand so you have good music to keep you motivated—I used to play lots of dance-type pop music to keep me in the mood to keep going. I can't even tell you how many workouts I would force myself to finish to the tune of "Gangnam Style." I liked working out when I was in my first semester because it got me out of the room, in a relatively social environment, and it would actually help me feel relaxed since I would usually come home, shower, and be able to sleep better during the night.

However, if you are athletic (and kudos to you if you are), you could always join a club or intramural sports team to practice and play with, much like sports in high school. These teams sometimes travel or are much more relaxed than you might be used to, but it gets your body moving!

If you are able to walk or bike to certain places on campus without taking a car or public transportation, by all means do it so you aren't completely sedentary. This should also help you tackle the "freshman 15" since you are moving your body in some sort of way, even if it's just walking to the student union or to class.

Transportation/travel

Depending on where you live or where you school is, transportation and/or travel are relevant topics for you. If you live at home and are a commuter student to a local college, you might get to school by driving or taking public transportation. It is up to you to plan accordingly to get to school on time: wake up, get dressed, eat breakfast, and get on the road before rush hour and be on time to your first class.

No matter how you are getting to class, make sure to leave depending on how long you think it will take to get there and how early you want to be there. I like to leave about 30 minutes before my class, so I am about ten minutes early. I think that is enough time in smaller courses to get a good seat, but when I was in large classes I would leave an hour early so I could sit wherever I wanted. If you are driving or taking a bus, make sure to build in the time it takes to get there. A bus might stop at every bus stop, there might be traffic, and other factors if you are driving or taking public transport.

When planning on large travel trips to go home on an airplane or a bus, you should plan far in advance, especially on major holidays. Follow all the rules, keep every email or mail sent to you from the travel agency or website, and make sure you do not leave any personal belongings behind. It is up to you to book trips far before the actual day so the trips are not full. We will be discussing more about this and going home in a later section though, so stay tuned!

To drive or not to drive

If you're commuting to school because you live at home or off-campus, you will probably be more likely to have a car than a student who does live on campus. Having a car on campus means finding parking, getting permits if needed, and dealing with student drivers who might be under the influence, irresponsible, or likely to hit your car. You need to also keep in mind the costs of gas, and upkeep and repairs if your car needs that. Start up your car each week so it does not die, even if you aren't driving often. You will also need to keep your license on you at all times. Having a car is a big responsibility, and if you are up for it, it can be very rewarding.

If you are not driving or you go to a school where freshmen are not allowed to have cars, your best asset will be having a friend who has a car, or knowing how to get around without a car. I did not have a car even though freshmen were allowed to. My roommate had a car—that was my logic, and I was always an anxious driver to begin with. I still am. I consider myself a good driver, but anxious. I also did not want to be the designated driver for anyone or have to take people places and get used for having a car. I do know that a lot of students with autism do not drive either, so you will have to get used to asking people to give you a ride if you want to go somewhere by car. However, I chose to become a master of walking anywhere within about two miles or taking public buses. I learned all the different routes to get to anywhere I would need to go, except for certain restaurants and large attractions. I learned to make do with what I had, and found walking and buses to be a more social experience that was better for me anyway, but sometimes I do find myself asking for rides as well.

Finances

Finance is a very scary concept as a young adult, especially if you're not too aware of the world around you and how much things cost. You might be on a budget, have student debt, just have a credit/debit card, or have a job and need to pay taxes. I am by no means a financial expert. I had a prepaid college plan so my tuition was paid for when I was in diapers. My parents pay for my dorm room and cover nearly all of my expenses by putting money into a student bank account for me. My dad does my taxes for my business, HaleyMossART, with his accountant and I haven't seen a tax form since high school when my beloved math teacher used to make us practice filling them out for Tax Day.

However, it is important to be responsible with money. Do not misplace your credit or debit cards, and if you do for any reason, tell your parents and report it to cancel your cards. It is good to establish credit when you are young if you are very responsible and capable of having a credit card. If you use an ATM, make sure to cover the keypad when you insert your PIN so you do not risk anyone seeing it and stealing your bank account information. Take out receipts as well so you know when you are depositing and withdrawing money from your account, and keep them somewhere safe. I also keep receipts whenever I pay with a credit card—especially if I give a gratuity on a restaurant bill so I can keep track and my parents know what I am spending when they get my bills.

You should always have some cash on you. I would recommend at least $20. That way, if any random expense comes up or you need money for a taxi or anything, you will be able to pay without risking giving up sensitive information such as a credit or debit card number. Keep that as safety money in your wallet at all times. If you do not like keeping a lot of money in your wallet but don't want to keep going to the ATM, store money in "safe places"—such as an extra couple bills in a purse or backpack, or in a good hiding place. That way you will always have emergency money no matter the situation.

If you are on a budget, keep it limited. For instance, if you have a certain amount of money per week, do not spend it all in the first day. You will need this money for food, meals, fun, gas if you have a car, and anything else out there—so using it all on fun the first day will not help you. You are supposed to manage what is given to you each week or month so you can survive and do not need to ask for more money or borrow.

Beware of friends when it comes to money. If you are lending to a friend, do not expect to get your money back. People will deny you lending them and it is incredibly awkward to ask them to pay you back. Also, you don't want to be the "rich friend" because you will be taken advantage of. You don't want to be paying for pizzas, dinner, or just excursions for fun.

I recently found a great online resource called Mint.com (www.mint.com). Mint helps you budget and allocate your money and keeps all of your financial data in one place with a friendly-looking interface and reminders. I think this could be good for us to learn with because it does seem fairly simple.

Safety

Safety when you have autism is an extra important thing to bring up, and I will be honest: as a young woman, I fear for my safety more than the guys out there. You're at a higher risk for sexual assault and other crimes, and all it takes is one creepy person to ruin your day. I take the topic of safety very seriously since I know I am a magnet for strange situations and people, so I will try my best to impart some of the knowledge I have learned from these encounters as well as basic safety tips.

My first basic safety tip for you is no matter where you go, have a cell phone on you. It is even better if you have a smart phone with GPS enabled in the event of an emergency so you could be easily located. With your cell phone, make sure you have an "in case of emergency" (ICE) list like I have in my iPhone—the ICE list has all sorts of important numbers. My ICE contact list has the phone numbers of the university's police department, my parents, my friend, and anyone I know who I could call and get help from in the event of an emergency or if I feel unsafe at any time. Your roommate would be a good addition to this list, too. If you do not have your local police phone number, I recommend looking it up online and saving it in your phone. I never had to call them, but I know I have the number in the event I ever have to. I would also add the number of a taxi company in case you feel safer taking a cab home for any reason.

I also highly advise not to go out alone at night. If you are out at night and are in fact alone, make sure you are going to and from somewhere with lots of people, even at night, so if something does happen you will be seen. Take the longer way home if it involves more crowded routes and well-lit paths and roads. I tend to stay near streetlights when I walk home at night because there are always cars, and bright lights. In case you're walking home at night alone, and there is a group nearby, don't be afraid to ask the group if you could walk with them until they get closer to your destination, or walk closely enough behind or in front of them that you blend in. That way, people will assume you are not alone. If you feel unsafe regardless of the circumstances, that is when you could use the ICE number for the taxi company you have and they could drive you home once you pay the fare.

Most of the creepy people I have encountered were on public city buses. I don't do anything special to attract attention. I purposely dress a little bit less nice if I am going on a city bus alone. I wear sweatpants, sunglasses, less makeup, or have my hair in a ponytail. I will do anything not to attract attention on these buses because honestly, some of the non-students are shady characters. I will never forget being on a half-hour bus ride to the grocery store, and this older guy (he had to be in his forties) would not stop staring at me. I noticed through my sunglasses he was staring and he wouldn't notice if I glanced back. When I got off the bus at the right stop, he told me I was really pretty, hence he couldn't stop looking at me. I waited until the bus left and I had all of my stuff to make sure I wasn't going to be followed. It was really weird. I also had another experience of chatting with someone and they asked me out. If you are riding a public bus, do not have your name anywhere on you, such as with a student ID on a lanyard around you neck, or invert your backpack if your initials are on it so they are not visible to the other passengers. A student ID or names give away the impression that you are young or naïve, or both, and could give a stranger a good reason to talk to you. You don't want to give out too much personal information to these people. I also learned after my two encounters to sit near the front of bus, as close to the driver as possible, so if any strange behavior took place, they could hear or notice it, or I could report it with ease.

If you're on a bus route that runs very frequently and a stranger is acting weirdly, get off at the next stop and wait for the next bus. I would only do this if you know the area and know how often the bus runs (don't do it if it is less than every 10–20 minutes so you are not stranded).

If you have a car and are driving, park in a well-lit part of the parking lot or closer to the store. I learned that a lot of assaults take place in parking lots, so you might as well minimize your risk there. Also, make sure that your car is locked and you take all valuables with them or hide them in the glove box or compartments within your car.

My next tip is safety for while you are at your dorm. You should not be letting people who don't live in your building inside, since that could be breaching the dorm's security system. If you are in your dorm room and do not expect or want any visitors, lock your door. If you are going to class for several hours, you should lock your door. If your door is unlocked, people will assume you're home, want visitors, or assume you are an easy target for burglary. Every on-campus theft my school had reported last semester occurred because someone left their door unlocked. If you are sleeping and don't want to be bothered, lock your door. If you live on a higher floor in your building, lock your windows as well. They probably are already locked, but there are people out there who try to break into windows while students are on holiday breaks or away.

This final tip may sound like an extreme tip, especially for some of you macho men and regular ladies, but if your university offers it, enroll in a self-defense class. Self-defense classes are available to college students at a low-cost, if not free, and are normally offered by an accredited organization or the police department. You shouldn't be afraid to take self-defense because of your athletic ability. I am one of the biggest couch potatoes, who was always picked last in gym class and could trip up the stairs, and I still was successful in completing a self-defense class and felt good about it. Self-defense not only teaches you wonderful safety tips if you don't have to punch, kick, and scream, and also teaches you how to pull off these techniques if you are kidnapped, or have some kind of scary situation such as being followed. It is very empowering, and also fun. A lot of people really enjoy it and some even do it together as a social activity. It is the only time you can actually fight with police officers and not get in trouble. It was pretty cool to pummel a male police officer twice my size after we learned the different methods of defending ourselves. I plan on going back to do self-defense review next semester because I found it that helpful to know how to protect myself from harm. However, my class was designed for women to defend themselves, so if you are a guy, you might want to make sure you're not trying to enroll in a women's class.

Health

I hope you listened to me when I said you should pack a "pharmacy" box full of important medications, band-aids, etc., because this is where we discuss health. You will probably get sick during your college career at least once. You might get a cold or flu because your immune system is weakened from all the stress of college life, or you might just have allergies. If your "pharmacy" isn't working or there is something more serious going on, make sure to check out your campus infirmary—a doctor or nurse there can help you out.

If you do get sick, make sure not to overdo it and rest accordingly while keeping up with class. Professors will demand a serious doctor's note if you missed a test or quiz without notice so make sure it's a real emergency before skipping out because of how you feel!

If your "pharmacy" box doesn't have the medicines you need, your campus probably has some sort of equivalent to the high school nurse's office (although it most likely has a fancier name, like an "infirmary"). These health care centers provide low-cost services to students, such as checkups, referrals, prescriptions for you to fill, etc. You can get screenings for certain diseases, such as STDs, pregnancy tests, birth control (pills, condoms, etc.), vaccines for the flu, and other important services far cheaper than a regular doctor's visit, or even for free. If you have a very serious injury or case that can't be treated while on campus, you might be referred to a nearby hospital; a teaching hospital if your campus has a medical school or its own hospital, or a county hospital. However, if you go to a hospital, beware of the complications with insurance, payments, and other stuff you might want to talk to your parents about before you leave for school.

I thankfully have never been sick enough while on campus to have to go to the infirmary, but I have visited their website just to see what is available to me in case I need anything. I recommend you do the same. I was actually going to get a flu vaccine during the spring since it was free for students, but the lines were over two hours long and I had a class to go to so I opted out. If you plan on waiting in line for a free vaccine or treatment like that, go early and think of how long you'd be willing to wait before committing to the line. Luckily I didn't get the flu. You might want vaccines for the flu or other sicknesses even more if you live in a dorm since you are in closer proximity to multiple people and there are probably a lot of germs! I've gotten my fair share of colds and stress sicknesses from being overwhelmed and living near people who were sick (when my roommate had a cold, no matter what I did it was inevitable that I would catch it too).

I'm not a doctor or a science student, but I can help provide some tips so you don't get sick or have to deal with a lot of the issues associated with it while in school! To avoid getting sick on campus, make sure to monitor your stress so it doesn't weaken your immune system. Dress appropriately for cold weather so you don't freeze. Stay away from people who are getting sick so you don't catch it. Wash your hands frequently, or carry hand sanitizer in your backpack. If you take some of these tidbits to heart, you could avoid staying in bed because of the flu, a cold, or just exhaustion-related sickness. It is up to you to feel your best!

A life without friends—feelings of isolation

I already told you guys how to avoid isolation in a previous chapter, but sometimes, isolation is inevitable. It was for me, and I tried my best to make friends and meet people. I lived alone during my spring semester, had more online classes so I could free up more time, and was still trying to find my place on campus. I found myself sometimes going entire weekends and days off without even leaving my dorm or talking to anyone. It eventually drove me crazy. I'd get really sad, anxious, or just tired because I had nothing to do or nowhere to go or nobody to see. This, my friends, is what isolation felt like.

However, if you feel isolated, I recommend you try not to do what I did. Get out of your room so at least you see people and don't create a prison for yourself. Go to the gym, even if it's for a half hour. Go study at the library instead. Go for a walk. Do something so you see people, see some sunshine, and get out of your room. You will instantly begin to feel better.

I felt better about being isolated if I had something to work towards. If I had a difficult class, I would channel more of the energy into getting an "A" in that class. If I wanted to draw new stuff, I would do that too. I would make goal lists for myself of things I wanted to accomplish that week, and work steadily towards them, whether it was calling people from home, drawing pictures, writing, or getting assignments done.

If you don't have friends or don't want friends, I'll tell you the best advice I've ever gotten: be your own best friend. Take yourself shopping, play a game, do something that you know you'd enjoy and have fun with that. You are also free of the drama brought about by friends, as well as some of the commitments. Have fun, love yourself, and do what you want—it is your life, and you could very well be the best friend you've always wanted!

CHAPTER 9

HOME AND GROWING UP

Parent perspective

I asked my mom and dad to help your parents out and tell you a little bit about what it's like being a parent of a college student on the autism spectrum, and how it is a big transition for parents, as well!

Raising a child with any form of disability is a challenge, as we all know. Raising a single child on the autism spectrum is like raising three neurotypical children all at once. I am assuming all of you parents out there have devoted your lives to your child's wellbeing and success. We have given them our all and have been there every step of the way from initial ASD diagnosis through high school graduation. Hopefully we have prepared them well for their next journey: college or university. I can personally write a whole book on this process but instead decided to provide you, the reader, with a brief list for getting you and your ASD young adult ready for his or her university transition.

One of the first things I need to mention is please don't be helicopter parents once your child is enrolled. They are adults now. We need to let them fly by themselves. This doesn't mean not to be involved. We need to be there for them, but don't call the Dean of Students for updates. We as parents need to take a back seat and I know that this is extremely difficult as most of us have been handholding for 18 years. By not being helicopter parents, we give our kids encouragement that we believe in them and this trust is empowering to them. It also means we did a great job parenting all of the years that now our kids can leave and break autism glass ceilings!

Another pearl would be to be a careful listener of your kid's thoughts and conversations as they give many clues as to what is really happening at school. My husband and I are always there with advice, unconditional love and guidance. When problems do arise at school, which they inevitably do, we are immediately accessible and ready to help with guidance and suggestions. However, we empower Haley to handle her own problems and make decisions incorporating our words of encouragement unless it is a safety issue.

Our children need to deal with the "real world" shortly and this is our last chance to supervise and instruct them before entering the hostile world where we won't always be available to help on a moment's notice.

Letting go of our "babies" is very difficult emotionally. I cried the entire trip home from the university, as I was constantly worrying about everything. On the other hand, my husband was incredibly overjoyed as he saw this as the culmination of years of hard work and sacrifice knowing the basic tools are in place for success.

We realized that this was no guarantee that things would work out. We continually worry on a daily basis about Haley's safety, happiness, daily interactions with peers and professors but we have learned to "let go" as this is the way to success and growth. We know you are going to walk by your child's bedroom and have many mixed feelings... however, these feelings of loneliness and anxiety will fade as time passes and success ensues as the days pass. You and your partner will learn to enjoy each other again and if you are single you will have time to explore new possibilities. Remember you will still talk to your child often, if not several times a day. Barring any safety issues or illness, the less you hear from them, the better things are going since they are busy and involved in the daily life of University like everyone else who is balancing homework, classes, laundry, parties, sporting events and clubs. The kids love when you send "care packages" from home. We usually send homemade goodies, personal trinkets and cards of encouragement.

Our children need to know that they are leaving home is a hard adjustment for parents as well. Abundant free time not consumed with the daily life of autism and its difficulties on a moment-by-moment basis leaves us trying to occupy our time with not thinking about what's going on at the University. We discovered the best thing we can do is the same advice we gave to our daughter. Take it one day at a time. We are just on the other side of the same coin.

In conclusion, we say be supportive every day! Send emoticon texts and just remind your child that you are always there emotionally if not physically. After all, we will always be their biggest advocates, allies and above all *parents*.

—*Rick and Sherry Moss, my parents*

Guidance from parents

I am beyond close to my parents. I talk to them every day when I'm away, and if I have the time or can't talk for very long, I call multiple times a day. I came home every other weekend my first semester. I took summer classes online so I could stay home for an extra four months. We're really close, and I am the only child, so having a good relationship with my parents is more than important.

Even though you are living away from home, your parents are a very valuable resource. They probably know you better than anyone else does. They know your strengths and weaknesses and love you unconditionally. They only want the best for you. Your parents should not be fighting your battles, but they will be able to help you look at things in a new way, understand the world around you, and support you.

College is very unpredictable. A lot of what happens is because of the people around you, rather than you being unpredictable. You can't predict or guarantee how you might have done on a hard exam, what kind of mood your roommate is in, if someone is being manipulative, how someone will take a breakup, etc. Everyone around you has emotions and feelings too, and it's very hard to predict them, whether it's from something you do or say, or another factor.

However, the unpredictability of other people is where your parents come in. Your parents are probably neurotypical people who don't have autism, and can understand these cues and emotions better than we can. If I'm unsure of how to act or what to do, I ask my parents. Back when I was younger, we'd script social scenarios so I would know what to do. Unfortunately though, young adults are harder to predict than younger kids whose parents your parents were also friends with or saw at school functions.

Your parents are still your guides. I called my parents asking for dating advice, roommate advice, ideas for what to get involved with, validation I was doing the right thing by living away, and countless other things. The guidance my parents were able to give me during my freshman year was invaluable. I was able to handle many things with that extra encouragement and scripting that I would have been completely lost on otherwise.

When you talk to your parents, and especially if you need advice, try to find private time to do this. You don't want your roommate listening in or others. Ask your roommate to respectfully leave if you want your space, or find an outdoor space with good cell reception so you can talk. If you're talking about someone you know when that person is around (such as your roommate)—come up with a code name or a code to use to say, "I would like to talk about so-and-so, but I can't right now."

Helicopter parents

As a person with autism, I know for a fact that my parents were once helicopter parents. Helicopter parents are the type of parents who monitor a lot of the things you do, worry often, and want to know pretty much everything. I know what it's like getting frantic phone calls if I forget to call back. I know that my parents are often worried sick about me. However, helicopter parents are not always the best when you're an adult and living on your own. When you lived at home, having those friendly reminders and everything working in your favor was great, but now that you're on your own, it's your time to shine as much as possible.

When you are living on your own, the idea is for you to become independent and take care of yourself. You should know how to make or get your own meals, shower and take care of personal hygiene, do your homework, and get enough sleep without your parents constantly reminding you. You want to give your parents hope and faith in how you are growing on your own. It is up to you to give them less of a reason to hover around like helicopters. Sure, they love you and will always worry, but you need to learn how to do many of these things yourself.

The main issue with helicopter parents in college comes down to academics and the adults you meet at college. Your parents simply can't call your professor and complain if you're not doing well, or if they want the professor to keep an eye out for you. Your parents can't call the Dean's office and ask how you're doing. In some places, your parents legally do not have access to your grades unless you sign a consent form. Your academic career is in your hands, and from a legal perspective, you can offer up whatever information you want to. If you go to counseling, everything you say (unless it could harm you or someone physically, such as a verbal threat), is confidential. These are common issues with regular parents too: my college even addressed all of this at a parent orientation session, so this happens far more than we think.

In order to keep your helicopter parents proud and happy, make sure to update them regularly (I call home daily, with the exception of midterms and finals), tell them how you are doing honestly, and give access to your transcripts and final grades. If your university has an extensive online program with hub pages for courses regardless of if they are in-person or not, you don't need to give your parents access to that—they shouldn't be taking your tests, doing your readings, or other assignments on your behalf since that is academic dishonesty a.k.a. cheating!

Coming home

I'll be honest: coming home is the highlight of my college career. I came home every two weeks for the first semester (after the first month passed by, and with the exception of midterms). I came home mainly because I wanted sleep (my roommate's sleep schedule affected me and would force me to stay awake longer than usual), privacy, quiet time, and well, I missed my family most importantly. It wasn't until I got home that I realized everything I missed about being home. When you're a teenager with autism and you want your independence and less of the helicopter parenting, going away from home seems really exciting. But the minute I come home, I feel like a happy child again. I miss having my mom do my laundry, having home-cooked meals, meals from my favorite local restaurants, petting my dog, getting to watch whatever I want on television while chilling on the couch, and just spending time with my family.

Coming home gets easier on everyone as you begin to do it more. My first couple trips back to college were emotionally rough on my family and I. They loved having me back, and sending me off alone was sad. I wanted to stay because I didn't want to go back to the stressful college life of roommates, papers, social obligations, exams, studying, and just being away from home. We never got used to me going away after coming home, but my mom and I became a bit less of crying wrecks after a few months of the cycle.

If you are planning on coming home when living far away, make sure to check your schedule to make sure you don't have an obligation at school for when you are home. If you are employed, make sure you request time off or do not have hours scheduled for when you want to go home. If you have an exam, don't try to reschedule it unless it's an emergency—go home after the exam. Make sure you don't have an unbearable workload to take care of when you are home by doing the work in advance, or saving enough work that you could do it on an airplane, train, or bus ride if that is how you choose to travel home. If your schedule looks clear to go home, it is time to book your trip or make other arrangements to get home.

If you live close enough to your college, you could drive home, carpool, or have your parents pick you up, but if you live far away, that isn't always the case. If you are going to be booking your trip, try to do it far enough in advance that you can get a ticket for a bus, train, or airplane. I find unpopular times (usually weekends) require less notice for booking—unpopular times to me are defined as times when large events are happening on campus, such as big sporting events like football games, parent and family weekends, or a weekend before major exams. With unpopular weekends you can get away with less notice to book tickets. However, popular times to travel are breaks such as homecoming, Thanksgiving, Winter Break, Spring Break, and the end of the spring semester for summertime. If you plan on going home during any of those five times (which nearly everybody does), book far in advance. I would start making those arrangements once you move into your dorm in the summer since Thanksgiving travel especially is very busy and very confusing.

When you come home, it will be very exciting. Your family will be very excited to see you, and want to hear about all they have missed. However, after a busy day of travel, you're probably going to be exhausted and might not be yourself. Give your family fair warning. Every single time I come home, I am exhausted beyond belief from sitting on a bus for five hours, so usually I just want to give everyone a hug, eat something, and relax by watching TV or getting some sleep. Your family might be aware that college is hard on you, so they might give you some space depending on your needs (in my case, I would sleep a lot when I came home, so I was allowed to sleep a lot later than

I used to while I lived at home). However, while you're home, make sure to do lots of fun things you miss about being home. If you miss playing video games, go play some video games. If you just miss watching movies with your family, watch movies with everyone. If you want to see certain people, make sure you have the time to spend with people outside of your family. I rarely if ever see friends from home while I'm home, unless it's for more than a week at a time. I usually come home on weekends (Friday night to Sunday afternoon), so I don't have much time to hang out with other people.

You're an adult now!

When you turn 18 in the US, you are legally an adult. You are no longer "owned" by your parents, and anything you do reflects on you. Once you are an adult, nearly everything begins to fall into your own hands. You can gamble, book vacations, get into adult venues, and do all sorts of cool-sounding adult stuff, but the most important thing that comes with being an adult is responsibility. I talked about how when you go to college you learn how to live independently and look after yourself, and most of all, advocate for yourself. Your parents love you and did the best for you, but now it is your turn to speak up for yourself and ensure your own success.

When I turned 18, I learned the importance of self-advocating. Advocating on your behalf is no longer your parents' jobs. I'm basically saying that it is up to you to talk to professors when you need help or you're doing poorly, to seek help from the correct people when needed, and to have no fear in standing up for yourself when it comes to other people. You are responsible for educating those who need to know about autism, or any other difficulties you may be facing, and making sure you get services, opportunities, and the guidance necessary to succeed. It is scary at first, but practice scripting these situations where you would be advocating for yourself with your parents or someone who understands so you can be prepared for when you are on your own and your parents can't help you nearly as much as they used to because simply, you are an adult, and it is now your responsibility and right to speak up for yourself, have things work for you, and evoke change around you.

The most important tip I have for you regarding self-advocacy is to be comfortable with yourself and your own diagnosis. If you embrace it and accept that it does not define you, but is a part of who you are, you will have better luck and more confidence when requesting services and meeting with people who can help you out in college as well as finding other programs to work with.

HELPFUL WEBSITES

www.amazon.com—If you are a college student with a .edu email address, sign up for a six-month subscription to get access to free two-day shipping on pretty much everything you buy.

www.commonapp.org—This is a place where you can submit multiple college applications in one place.

www.mint.com—Here, you can track your money, how much you are spending, and get notifications about your habits to help you manage your finances.

www.pinterest.com—This is great for ideas for outfits and things that are cool in dorms, etc.

INDEX